THE COST OF DISCIPLESHIP

Making Disciples In Turbulent Times
2 Timothy 2:2 Discipling 101

CHARLES W MORRIS

Copyright © 2022 Charles W Morris

All rights reserved. No part of this book may be used or reproduced by any means, graphic, electronic, or mechanical, including photocopying, recording, taping, or by any information storage retrieval system without the written permission of the publisher except in the case of brief quotations embodied in critical articles and reviews.

Scriptures are taken from the English Standard Version of the Bible

Books may be ordered through booksellers or by contacting:
RSIP
Raising the Standard International Publishing L. L. C.
https://www.rsipublishing.com

RSIP-Charles Morris
https://www.rsiministry.com
Navarre, Florida
ISBN: 9781955830911

Printed in the United States of America
Edition Date: November 2022

TABLE OF CONTENTS

1	Introduction	1
2	Why Do We Need A Mentorship Plan?	10
3	The Commitment To Be Mentored Or Discipled	18
4	To Be A Disciple Of The Lord Jesus Christ, There Must Be A Commitment To Forsake Family Ties For Christ	23
5	To Be A Disciple Of The Lord Jesus Christ, There Must Be A Commitment To "Death To Self" And To Following Christ	31
6	To Be A Disciple Of The Lord Jesus Christ, There Must Be A Commitment Toward Faithfulness	40
7	To Be A Disciple Of The Lord Jesus Christ, There Must Be A Commitment Towards Loving The Lord Jesus Christ And Loving One Another	49
8	To Be A Disciple Of The Lord Jesus Christ, There Must Be A Commitment Toward Spiritual Hunger And Thirst	56
9	To Be A Disciple Of The Lord Jesus Christ, There Must Be A Commitment To Having A Teachable Attitude	63
10	To Be A Disciple Of The Lord Jesus Christ, There Must Be A Commitment To Take On	74

	The Yoke Of Our Lord Jesus Christ	
11	The Cost Of Developing Others Into Leadership	77
12	Marks Of An Ideal Mentor	79
13	How Do I Find A Mentor For Me	81
14	What Is My Responsibility As A Trainee Or "Protégé"	83
15	Dealing With Conflict Or Disagreement In The Mentoring Process	87
16	How To Make The Time You Need	89
	More Books By Charles Morris	96
	About The Author	100

THE COST OF DISCIPLESHIP

-1-
INTRODUCTION

As a boy, Michelangelo presented himself to a master sculptor to be his pupil. The old master sculptor said to the young Michelangelo, "This will take all of your life." Michelangelo replied, "What else is life for?" Although just a young boy, Michelangelo knew that for life to have any real meaning, one must be committed to something. We have heard the old cliché "Aim at nothing, and you will hit it every time." A person who is not committed to something or someone will live an empty life.

When I was in high school, in the eleventh grade, I had a friend who kept professing that he would be a millionaire by the time he was 25 years old. These statements came in 1971, and since I came from a low-income family, I couldn't even imagine having ten thousand dollars, much less a million dollars. I laughed at him and called him a dreamer. I left home for the military and lost track of my high school friend. In 2009 my high school friend and I reconnected after not seeing each other for close to 37 years. He told me he had gotten married, which slowed his progress, but he was a millionaire by age 35. He had a dream and goal, and he purposed his life toward it. Since becoming a millionaire, he became born again and is active in missions and church planting in many different countries. So, I echo Michelangelo's words regarding serving and growing in our Lord Jesus Christ. "What else is life for?"

Discipleship! A tremendous Biblical word that has taken a bad rap over the years and is often underestimated in its impact on a person and a church. I will interchange the terms discipleship and mentoring throughout this study to show the connection and cost of being a disciple and discipling of others. I want to start this study with my "mentoring motto." This motto will be the theme in all I say in this study, so keep it in mind as you read "The Cost Of Discipleship."

**Mentoring is not just about giving away knowledge,
But the giving away of our lives.
What else is life for?**

Before going any further, let me say this study is not the final word on mentoring the believer to become a disciple. I hope and pray that the reader will continue the lifelong endeavor of becoming a disciple and, in turn, teaching all things that the Father has revealed in the growing process to others.

Some Bible teachers state that you are a disciple once you receive the Lord Jesus Christ as Savior. However, according to the Word of God, this is not true and cheapens the call to maturity. Giving one's life to the Lord for salvation is the race's starting point but not the entire race. Once we are saved, we must commit our lives to the Lord Jesus Christ as our Teacher and learn to sit at His feet, hear His voice, and be made disciples.

We certainly live in turbulent times. The economy is unstable, with inflation skyrocketing. There is civil and political unrest with wars and rumors of wars. The news reports reveal lawlessness unleashed in every corner of the world. If ever we needed stable, mature Christians taking their rightful place as spiritual moms and dads, we need it now. Our young believers stand the chance of getting caught in the cultural wave of amoral madness and progressive universalism. We need mentors to take their place and be willing to accept the cost of discipleship.

Mentoring is an excellent investment in time, energy, and resources and well worth our desiring after. But it cost something, which we will get into later in the book. If you knew me, you would know that one of my favorite phrases is, "we need to begin with the end in mind." My favorite Scripture passage for this is 2 Timothy 2:2.

> **2 Timothy 2:2 ESV and what you have heard from me in the presence of many witnesses entrust to faithful men who will be able to teach others also.**

This Scripture says that mentoring is genuinely taking place when we see people being mentored by those we mentor while we are being mentored. Now that is a mouth full, so let's break it down. We are being trained and discipled while teaching and discipling others, who are, in turn, training and discipling others. It is a generational progressive discipleship process. Somewhere along the line, we have failed the Biblical progression the Apostle Paul gave us in 2 Timothy 2:2.

Mentoring or discipling is a responsibility for all of us. We are all called to minister the truth that is in us to others. This study is filled with Scriptural references relating to the mentoring process. Read these and ask the Lord for someone to pour your life into and if you don't have it, pray for someone who will pour their life into you.

> **Matthew 28:19-20 (ESV) Go therefore and make disciples of all nations, baptizing them in the name of the Father and of the Son and of the Holy Spirit, 20 teaching them to observe all that I have**

commanded you. And behold, I am with you always, to the end of the age."

As we go, we need to make disciples. How? Win the lost, teach them to follow the Lord in "believer's baptism," and then teach them to obey everything the Lord taught the disciples.

We should pray. We need to pray. Therefore PRAY! We should preach. We need to preach. Therefore PREACH! However, our maturity does not happen through prayer and hearing sermons. The reverse is true. Our prayer life becomes more effective as we mature. Teaching and preaching the gospel message to others become more effective as we grow.

The people we pray for and preach to do not mature because of our prayers and preaching. Did you get this? We cannot preach or pray people into maturity. Let me jump on this bandwagon for a minute. I have pastored for over 45 years. When starting out, I actually believed the delusion that I was everyone's pastor in the church I ministered. It took years to understand that I may have been everyone's preacher, but there was no way I could be everyone's pastor. Our Lord Jesus pastored only twelve. He taught thousands of people the Word of God, but He poured His life only into the twelve disciples who followed Him for three years. Why is this? I will cover this in detail in chapter 16 when I address the time issue.

People need prayer and the Word, and we should continue doing it, but there must be a maturing or discipling process in place. We all have to pay the price to become mature disciples of our Lord.

No one gets to be mature through a microwave process. If this were not true, the Lord would not have commanded us to "make disciples." If preaching or praying alone would have made disciples, then we would have been instructed in the Word about how to pray and preach to produce disciples. If the praying and preaching methods were enough, we could eliminate spiritual, biblical teachers. Again, I cannot emphasize enough the importance of praying, and teaching and preaching the Word of God. So, don't stop doing it. But don't use it to replace mentoring people and making disciples.

It is understood that we pray more effectively and preach more substance as we mature. It is like a baby making noises as he tries to form words. As he develops more and more, the noises start to make sense to the hearer. The baby starts crying when he is hungry for milk. We don't always know why he cries because he could be hungry, wet, tired, or just wants to be held. Therefore, when the baby cries, we do the "hit and miss" process to comfort him. We check his diaper to ensure that he is okay there. We hold him to see if he just wants some physical cuddle time. Then we try the bottle of milk. By the time he is two years old, he just asks for milk. As he becomes able to communicate his needs, there is no question about what he wants.

The same is true of Bible study when it is by itself. Bible study alone will not transform our lives. It will not give us power, peace, joy, comfort, hope, and a number of other gifts God longs for us to use and enjoy. Bible study is vitally important and should be done regularly and faithfully. Through Bible study, we can grow in our understanding of the Lord, His kingdom, and our place in it.

These things are essential, but we need more. We need to rely on the Holy Spirit to guide us, guide our study, and show our application of the Bible's truths. The letter of the law by itself is death. We need to regularly meet the author of the Book in order to mature in the understanding and purpose of the Book. One of the great promises of the Word teaches us that one of the ministering works of the Holy Spirit is to guide us and teach us all things.

> ***John 14:26 ESV But the Helper, the Holy Spirit, whom the Father will send in my name, he will teach you all things and bring to your remembrance all that I have said to you.***
>
> ***Matthew 10:19-20 ESV When they deliver you over, do not be anxious how you are to speak or what you are to say, for what you are to say will be given to you in that hour. (20) For it is not you who speak, but the Spirit of your Father speaking through you.***
>
> ***2 Corinthians 3:5-11 ESV (5) Not that we are sufficient in ourselves to claim anything as coming from us, but our sufficiency is from God, (6) who has made us sufficient to be ministers of a new covenant, not of the letter but of the Spirit. For the letter kills, but the Spirit gives life. (7) Now if the ministry of death, carved in letters on stone, came with such glory that the Israelites could not gaze at Moses' face because of its glory, which was being brought to an end, (8) will not the ministry of the Spirit have even more glory? (9) For if there was glory in the ministry of condemnation, the ministry of righteousness must far exceed it in glory. (10) Indeed, in this case, what once had glory has come to have no glory at all, because of the glory that surpasses it. (11) For if what was being brought to an end came with glory, much more will what is permanent have glory.***

> *1 Corinthians 2:12-15 ESV (12) Now we have received not the spirit of the world, but the Spirit who is from God, that we might understand the things freely given us by God. (13) And we impart this in words not taught by human wisdom but taught by the Spirit, interpreting spiritual truths to those who are spiritual. (14) The natural person does not accept the things of the Spirit of God, for they are folly to him, and he is not able to understand them because they are spiritually discerned. (15) The spiritual person judges all things, but is himself to be judged by no one.*
>
> *1 John 2:20 ESV But you have been anointed by the Holy One, and you all have knowledge.*

In July 2011, a few Pastors from Pennsylvania asked me about my leadership ideas and methodology. I realized that I had taught a lot about spiritual leadership, but I did not have much written down for others to read. Therefore, I set out to compile years of notes for leadership teaching. First, I want to say that this teaching, although seemingly long, is by far not the final word nor complete in content. As I experience more about the leading and mentoring process, more will be added. Before teaching the principles of leadership, I will give what I believe to be a Biblical definition of authentic leadership.

ASSIGNMENTS

My mentor, the late Pastor Peter Lord, talked a lot about going to the doctor for a checkup. Then he used that to establish a check-up on himself and those he mentored. He called it "giving himself and others a spiritual exam." We will be doing this throughout this book. Why? Do you remember the old FRAM oil filter commercial that says, "You can thank me now or pay me later?" It was on the premise that regular oil changes would save the life of your engine. The same is valid with proper mentorship or discipleship. It operates under the assumption of "soul care." Once you are saved, it is better to thank someone for their daily watch-care over your soul than pay to get fixed when broken.

If we genuinely want to serve God's people, which is the church or body of our Lord Jesus Christ, in spiritual leadership, we need to learn some basics about faithfulness. I pray that this will guide and assist us all in developing sensitivity to the promptings of the Holy Spirit in our lives as He guides us into a fruitful leadership ministry and proper mentoring of the saints.

Like all of my studies, many Scriptures will be given in this study. I do this because what our heavenly Father says in His Word exceeds anything I can possibly say about the subject of making a disciple and the cost of discipleship. I strongly suggest that the reader do as the Bereans did in Acts 17:10-11. The Bereans received the word from the Apostles with an open mind and then went back and searched the Scriptures daily to prove that the Apostles' doctrine was correct.

> ***Acts 17:10-12 ESV** The brothers immediately sent Paul and Silas away by night to Berea, and when they arrived they went into the Jewish synagogue. (11) Now these Jews were more noble than those in Thessalonica; they received the word with all eagerness, examining the Scriptures daily to see if these things were so. (12) Many of them*

therefore believed, with not a few Greek women of high standing as well as men.

WE MUST DISCERN WAYS WE MAY ENCOURAGE FAITH IN THE HEARTS OF THE PEOPLE WE LEAD

Make clear what it means to lead God's people in the manner He would have them to be led. We need to know how to rely totally on the anointing of the Holy Spirit and be open and approachable to others. We must encourage others and ourselves in the faith to believe in God for miracles, signs, and wonders manifested among the people we serve.

As we pursue this study in leadership and the cost of discipleship, not only should we do so with the heart attitude of being humbled and challenged, but we should also be grateful to God for the opportunity to serve in His kingdom.

-2-
WHY DO WE NEED A MENTORSHIP PLAN?

It should go without saying that most believers are not as mature in their faith as they think they are. They may seem mature until faced with an issue or crisis. When tribulation and trials come, the fruit reveals the root. When we are squeezed, that which is within us comes out. The things which come out of our mouths show our heart condition.

The term "discipleship" has taken a bad hit recently and has come to be regarded as old school, dated, and no longer relevant to modern-day Christianity. That which is a priority within the Scriptures should be a priority to us. When we were saved, we were adopted into the family of God as children of the King of Glory. We were not adopted as spiritual adults but as newborn babies. Therefore, we need a spiritual growth plan like a physical growth plan when we are born. Aim at nothing, and we will hit it every time. We must be intentional in our spiritual growth and the mentoring of others.

MAKING DISCIPLES IS MATURING BELIEVERS IN THE LORD

- Not all Believers are mature in the Faith.
- Not all Believers are mature in the Word.
- Not all Believers are mature in their Walk.
- Not all Believers are mature in their Talk.
- Not all Believers are mature in their Thoughts.

Our primary Scripture in this study will be 2 Timothy 2:2.

2 Timothy 2:2. ESV and what you have heard from me in the presence of many witnesses entrust to faithful men who will be able to teach others also.

There is a cost to discipleship. I can't receive what I don't think I need and can't give what I don't possess. Our objective is to assist the reader in understanding how mature they are personally and how to continue to "grow up in the Lord and the Word." To assist the reader in the importance of establishing mentor relationships for the purpose of discipling others is paramount. This book is an unapologetic approach from the Scriptures to the application of truth by the individual for the purpose of making disciples. We live in days when the Christian is bombarded with the ideology of tolerance and compromise with people desiring to have their ears tickled with a soft, watered-down Gospel.

SPIRITUAL LEADERS HAVE THE MANDATE TO DISCIPLE THE SAINTS

When we think about maturity, we would naturally go to Apostle Paul's mandate in Ephesians 4:11-16 in seeing that the call of our heavenly Father is for the body of Christ to come into full maturity and unity of faith.

Ephesians 4:11-16 ESV And he gave the apostles, the prophets, the evangelists, the shepherds and teachers, (12) to equip the saints for the work of ministry, for building up the body of Christ, (13)

until we all attain to the unity of the faith and of the knowledge of the Son of God, to mature manhood, to the measure of the stature of the fullness of Christ, (14) so that we may no longer be children, tossed to and fro by the waves and carried about by every wind of doctrine, by human cunning, by craftiness in deceitful schemes. (15) Rather, speaking the truth in love, we are to grow up in every way into him who is the head, into Christ, (16) from whom the whole body, joined and held together by every joint with which it is equipped, when each part is working properly, makes the body grow so that it builds itself up in love.

WE WILL FACE FALSE DOCTRINES

False doctrines will come as doctrines of demons, doctrines of men, and doctrines of religion. People will become emotionally and mentally tied to these false doctrines and turn away from sound Biblical teaching.

2 Timothy 4:3-4 ESV For the time is coming when people will not endure sound teaching, but having itching ears they will accumulate for themselves teachers to suit their own passions, (4) and will turn away from listening to the truth and wander off into myths.

Without reservation, this author stands against the doctrine of universalism, the false teachings that corrupt God's love and judgment, and any teaching that waters down or denies the blood atonement and Deity of our Lord Jesus Christ. These false doctrines include, but are not limited to:

THE COST OF DISCIPLESHIP

    A. Moral Government Theology (Mgt) Doctrine:
    B. Ultimate Reconciliation Doctrine:
    C. Jesus Died Spiritually (JDS) Doctrine:
    D. Humanistic Theology or Ideology
    E. Gnosticism

This author states what the Bible claims. There is no way to God, heaven, and eternal life except by faith in the Son of God, the Lord Jesus Christ, who is Deity Himself. The cross was not a loss but a victory.

> **John 14:6 ESV Jesus said to him, "I am the way, and the truth, and the life. No one comes to the Father except through me.**
>
> **Acts 4:11-12 ESV This Jesus is the stone that was rejected by you, the builders, which has become the cornerstone. (12) And there is salvation in no one else, for there is no other name under heaven given among men by which we must be saved."**
>
> **1 Peter 3:18 ESV For Christ also suffered once for sins, the righteous for the unrighteous, that he might bring us to God, being put to death in the flesh but made alive in the spirit,**

We state that God is not doing a "new thing" but doing what He has always done, even though it may be new to us. We note that much of the church's modern-day "new revelation" is nothing more than renaming "new age" teachings, humanism, and universalism. This author embraces the need for the baptism with the Holy Spirit, daily walking in the fullness of the Spirit, and rightly dividing the Word of God individually and within the body of Christ.

We live in a time where it is imperative that we grow up spiritually after salvation. For way too long now, many believers have been satisfied with what is called "fire insurance Christianity" and have not been diligent in growing up in the faith. The statement "fire insurance Christianity" means that there are people who came under the conviction of the Holy Spirit and called upon the name of the Lord Jesus Christ to be saved and have not gone any farther in their Christian growth. They are saved to eternal life if they stay in the faith and protected from the fire of hell (fire insurance) if they remain in the faith. Therefore, they assume to be content with their limited Christian growth. However, we are called to "grow up" as believers and to move from faith to faith, grace to grace, and glory to glory in a constant state of renewing the new man and putting off the old man. This author will also say by observation and experience that the average Christian assumes that they are more spiritual and mature than they actually are.

> **Ephesians 4:22-24 ESV to put off your old self, which belongs to your former manner of life and is corrupt through deceitful desires, (23) and to be renewed in the spirit of your minds, (24) and to put on the new self, created after the likeness of God in true righteousness and holiness.**
>
> **Romans 1:17 ESV For in it the righteousness of God is revealed from faith for faith, as it is written, "The righteous shall live by faith."**
>
> **John 1:16 ESV For from his fullness we have all received, grace upon grace.**

THE COST OF DISCIPLESHIP

2 Corinthians 3:18 ESV And we all, with unveiled face, beholding the glory of the Lord, are being transformed into the same image from one degree of glory to another. For this comes from the Lord who is the Spirit.

Romans 12:3 ESV For by the grace given to me I say to everyone among you not to think of himself more highly than he ought to think, but to think with sober judgment, each according to the measure of faith that God has assigned.

KNOW WHERE YOU ARE SPIRITUALLY

If we want to drive somewhere, there are two things we need to know before starting to drive. First, we need to know precisely where we are currently positioned, and second, we need to know where we want to go. So, it is with being made a disciple. We need to know where we are spiritually today, and we need to know where we are headed or our final destination.

The trip to becoming a spiritual mentor or a disciple is neither a quick trip nor a straight trip without a few detours and stops. The road to salvation is straight and narrow, but becoming a disciple has valleys, mountaintops, and wilderness places.

Debby and I often visited the Amish when we lived in Pennsylvania. Each Amish family specialized in one area of expertise. One family made furniture, another made cheese and butter, another made quilts, and so forth. We began to learn the last names of some of the Amish families and what particular article they specialized in. One day I remember being at an Amish family and asked how to get to the Toyer family. The Toyers built furniture, and I wanted a hickory rocker built. The response to the question I received has remained with me for over 25 years. The Amish gentleman replied, "you can't get there from here."

The Amish families rode in horse-drawn buggies, and it took a lot of time to go from one place to another. Therefore, they would leave their farm and go to the next closest farm. They would stop for a while and then head out to the next farm and stop there. This routine was repeated until they finally arrived at the farmhouse, which was their original aim. If they were at the Miller's farm and wanted to go to the Toyer's farm, they would travel from the Millers to the Yoders to the Hochstetlers and then to the Toyers. That is why they answer, "you can't get there from here." If they wanted to get to the Toyers, they had to get there from many stops.

Now let's bring this into becoming a spiritual mentor or disciple. I want to say, "we can't get there from here." We can get there from somewhere else, but we can't get there from here. The cost of discipleship is a process of moving from one place to another, where each move takes time and effort. I have had those I was mentoring move from one spiritual, emotional, or mental place to another. With each move, they thought they had arrived at being a disciple and were ready to quit the mentoring process. However, they only accomplished one leg of the journey and had not reached their destination.

This incomplete process has been a problem in many churches over the years. A person is witnessed to concerning Christ and becomes saved. They then go down into the waters of baptism and join the church. That is it. The next stage is to sit on their blessed assurance, hoping that Jesus will come soon to take them to heaven. Far too many people feel that they have arrived spiritually after being born again. The only thing left for them to do the rest of their lives is to attend church and tithe. How sad that this is what is being communicated directly or indirectly to believers in our churches. We need to evaluate where we are as leaders, mentors, and trainees and then determine where we want to go.

We all have our thoughts about what a disciple is. Some would say you are a disciple when you first become a Christian. Some would say you are a disciple once you have been saved for a certain number of years. Some would say you are a disciple once you reach a certain physical age. This study helps identify what the Word of God calls a disciple and reveals the fruit and traits of a true Biblical disciple. So, my friend, welcome to the journey of spiritual life.

Be ready. Although salvation was a free gift by faith through the grace of God, discipleship cost you your life.

-3-
THE COMMITMENT TO BE MENTORED OR DISCIPLED

Here is the thing about being a leader. A leader leads. I know, that's deep. But if a leader leads, then there must be someone following. Again, deep waters. Here is the catch. If you think you are a leader and don't have someone to your right, left, or behind you, you are not leading; you are just out for a walk. If we are going to be leaders and mentors, we need to find those who desire to be disciples. Remember, leaders. If we are to disciple young believers, we need to do so from the narrow path of God's righteousness.

COMMITTING TO BEING A DISCIPLE OF THE LORD JESUS CHRIST

I assume that the majority of the readers of this study are already saved and are in a position of training in order to come to the full knowledge of the Son of God into maturity, as stated in Ephesians 4:13. God the Father has placed certain defined "mandates" upon people within His Word. Obviously, the first mandate is a call to be born again. The second mandate is to become a disciple of our Lord Jesus Christ. Somehow this second mandate has been lost in the Church body, and many believe they are both a Christian and a disciple once they are saved. This principle is not valid. Many also believe that once saved, they can just somehow slide into being a disciple by virtue of longevity. This principle is also not true. Some spiritual babies have been saved for 30 or 40 years or longer. There must be a willingness and a process in place to be made into a disciple. We are **BORN AGAIN** to become Christians. However, we are **MADE** into disciples of our Lord Jesus Christ. A Christian is not made, and a disciple is not born.

The New Testament uses the Greek word "Mathetes" for the English word disciple. Strong's NT Concordances definition of "Mathetes" (Greek #3101) means "a learner or pupil." The Greek word "Matheteuo" (Greek #3100) means "to become a pupil, to enroll as a scholar, to teach, or to instruct." But as we will see in the Scriptures, being a disciple is much more than our idea of being a student or pupil who goes to a classroom or to listen and accumulate academics.

Becoming a disciple of the Lord Jesus Christ should be a goal sought by every believer. Being a disciple is not automatic because someone becomes "born again" or has been a believer and Church member for several years. Becoming a disciple of the Lord Jesus Christ carries certain pre-conditions and life choices. Just like there is the evidence of the fruit of the Holy Spirit to reveal a true Christian, there is Biblical evidence or fruit that indicates a true disciple of the Lord Jesus Christ. In fact, there is a list of attributes that our Lord gave concerning being a disciple.

I remember going to "discipleship training," where I learned certain truths about Bible disciplines such as reading the Word, praying, witnessing, and giving. I always wondered in these classes, "How many discipleship classes does one need to attend before becoming a disciple?" Have you ever wondered about this?

Discipleship classes should give us knowledge of the disciplines or mandates of the Christian life, which leads to becoming a disciple. However, the lessons could just be more mental assent which leads nowhere. We can become like the Bible verse which says, "Ever learning but not able to come to the knowledge of the truth."

> **2 Timothy 3:7 ESV   always learning and never able to arrive at a knowledge of the truth.**

BIBLICAL QUALIFICATIONS TO BE A DISCIPLE

Of course, there will be many who are not interested in being a disciple. The cost is beyond what they are willing to pay to be a Biblical disciple. Therefore, they either just assume the title of a disciple without considering the qualifications or consequences, or they ignore the term altogether. Some believers will "dummy down" the Biblical mandates in order to call themselves a disciple by seeking to take the path of least resistance.

Some believers are satisfied with more "head knowledge" of the Bible without considering the application of spiritual truths. Some think that mental assent to Biblical truths is discipleship. We should seek to know God's Word intellectually to renew our minds, but the Scriptures tell us to hide the Word in our hearts. We should cry out, "Write the Word on my heart, Lord."

If we truly desire to be a disciple, who in turn will disciple others, we need to know there is a price to pay. Salvation was free, but discipleship will cost you your life. Without pretexts in making Scriptures say something they don't, I have let the Word of God speak for itself. The traits of a true disciple are offensive to many who want to be called one without fulfilling the qualifications. Read the Scriptures given and ask the Father to show you your heart.

THE COST OF DISCIPLESHIP

Everyone needs discipled in some area. As you read, pray about who you are willing to place your life under to be your mentor. Then ask the Father to show you who you are to mentor.

A lake stays clean when it has an input of clean water, an outlet, and a no-dumping sign. Be faithful to receive what the Father gives, and then be faithful to give to other faithful men what was imparted to you. Let's look at some characteristics of the person who desires to be a disciple or mentored, and the cost required. I made the following statements in the introduction. Let's reread them.

The people we pray for and preach to do not mature because of our prayers and preaching. Did you get this? We cannot preach or pray people into maturity. Let me jump on this bandwagon for a minute. I have pastored for over 45 years. When starting out, I actually believed the delusion that I was everyone's pastor in the church I ministered. It took years to understand that I may have been everyone's preacher, but there was no way I could be everyone's pastor. Our Lord Jesus pastored only twelve. He taught thousands of people the Word of God, but He poured His life into the twelve that followed Him for three years. Why is this? I will address some of the answers here, but the time issue is covered in detail in chapter 16.

When a pastor goes to a new church, it is only natural to want to be everyone's pastor. But let's be realistic. We do not have the time, energy, or resources to pastor 50, 100, or 1,000 people. The max that we can effectively pastor is twelve. To truly pastor someone is to pour your life into them. This decision takes a great deal of time and commitment. We are deceiving ourselves if we think we are pastoring if all we are doing is preaching to someone twice a week and visiting them in times of sickness or death.

Since the mid-1990s, I have tried to "find my twelve." They may be scattered worldwide, but I have tried to maintain between two to twelve men I am discipling and effectively pastoring. For everyone else under my ministry, I preach, teach, and counsel as I have the opportunity to do so. It does not cost me much to prepare a sermon to preach, and it certainly does not cost the church member much to attend and listen to my message. Preaching or teaching a message in a church service is by far the least effective form of mentorship, but it will be the only opportunity allotted to us. There is little cost and commitment to each party, with little or no assessment or accountability to determine growth.

-4-
TO BE A DISCIPLE OF THE LORD JESUS CHRIST, THERE MUST BE A COMMITMENT TO FORSAKE FAMILY TIES FOR CHRIST

Cost #1: Forsake Family Ties

The Luke 14:25-27 passage is one of the most challenging hurdles to overcome for many Christians who read the Scriptures. It is a major trend among Christians to abandon Biblical truth concerning false holidays that are embraced as "Christian celebrations" because of emotional family ties. There is this false sense of Godly duty and righteousness if we forsake everything, even our Biblical convictions, for the sake of our family.

Taking a stand for truth and going after the heart of the Father is not easy when it comes to the pressure of family ties. I know of one church split where the "old money" of the church pressured their children and grandchildren to follow them in the split, or they would take their family members out of their will. Many children and grandchildren felt that the elder parents and grandparents were wrong spiritually and doctrinally. However, they gave in and forsook the truth because of pressure from family members. The pressure of possibly being left without an inheritance was too great a cost to pay for what they believed to be true. In other words, they had a price and were bought with it.

> ***Matthew 10:34-38 ESV** "Do not think that I have come to bring peace to the earth. I have not come to bring peace, but a sword. (35) For I have come to set a man against his father, and a daughter against her mother, and a daughter-in-law against her mother-in-law. (36) And a person's enemies will be those of his own household. (37) Whoever loves father or mother more than me is not worthy of me, and whoever loves son or daughter more than me is not worthy of me. (38) And whoever does not take his cross and follow me is not worthy of me.*
>
> ***Luke 14:25-26 ESV** Now great crowds accompanied him, and he turned and said to them, (26) "If anyone comes to me and does not hate his own father and mother and wife and children and brothers and sisters, yes, and even his own life, he cannot be my disciple.*

Having served as a Pastor for over forty years has given me the saddening opportunity to witness many believers walk away from the truths and blessings of God over the influence of family members or friends. This Luke 14:25-26 Scripture teaches us to be weaned from and be willing to walk away from all comforts in our life, including the ease of relationship, family, family name, and family inheritance. If we learn these Scriptures, we will learn to be constant, sincere, and willing to make the ultimate sacrifices as God leads us through life. These Scriptures are not telling us to hate our family literally.

This first demand for becoming a disciple may seem shocking and even staggering that our Lord would demand such a thing. If you attempt to explain away Luke 14:25-26 in some manner as to say that God did not mean what He said,

THE COST OF DISCIPLESHIP

then you are not ready to be considered a candidate for discipleship.

The word "Hyperbole" is a transliteration of a Greek word that means an exaggeration for effect but not to be taken literally. The word "hate" in verse 26 is used as a hyperbole. Our Lord uses the same word structure in Matthew chapters 5 and 18 concerning the cutting off our hands or plucking out our eyes. He did not intend for us to cut off our hands or pluck out our eyes, but the exaggerated text reveals the seriousness of the subject matter.

> **Matthew 5:29-30 ESV** *If your right eye causes you to sin, tear it out and throw it away. For it is better that you lose one of your members than that your whole body be thrown into hell. (30) And if your right hand causes you to sin, cut it off and throw it away. For it is better that you lose one of your members than that your whole body go into hell.*

> **Matthew 18:8-9 ESV** *And if your hand or your foot causes you to sin, cut it off and throw it away. It is better for you to enter life crippled or lame than with two hands or two feet to be thrown into the eternal fire. (9) And if your eye causes you to sin, tear it out and throw it away. It is better for you to enter life with one eye than with two eyes to be thrown into the hell of fire.*

Our Lord Jesus Christ is not telling us to despise or hate our families in Luke 14:25-27, but they are Scriptures of comparison between our love for God and our love for family. Our love for things and family should look like hate compared to our love for our Lord Jesus Christ. Our love for our own life should look like hate compared to our love for God. Suppose this proper relationship with God is not a reality of the heart. In that case, our decisions will be influenced by our family members, friends, or our personal desires instead of the Word, the will, and the character of God.

    He is not telling us to leave our families physically. But if the situation arose where we had to choose between following Christ or following a family member, the decision should have already been made for our Lord. This trait of being a disciple comes at a great cost. This decision would be a real struggle for a believer who has not been made into a disciple. Family or "blood relative" will come first over the way, will, and Word of God. As an example of this love relationship, I use peanut butter to describe my love. I love peanut butter, and I love my wife and children. But the love for my wife and children cannot be compared to peanut butter.

    Compared to my love for my wife and children, my love for peanut butter looks like hate. Abraham was called to leave his home, family, and country to follow our heavenly Father. This same illustration must be applied as the love for our family is compared to our Heavenly Father and Lord Jesus Christ.

> **Genesis 12:1-3 ESV Now the LORD said to Abram, "Go from your country and your kindred and your father's house to the land that I will show you. (2) And I will make of you a great nation, and I will bless you and make your name great, so that you will be a blessing. (3) I will bless those who bless you, and him who dishonors you I will curse, and in you all the families of the earth shall be blessed."**

THE COST OF DISCIPLESHIP

The Scriptures state in Matthew 10:34-38 that because of our faith in the Lord Jesus Christ, some of our household members will become our greatest enemies. Not everyone who is a family member will come and sit at the table of the Lord. Therefore, we are called to go out and gather others so that the table is full. Basically, Luke 14 teaches that many are called, but few are chosen.

> **Luke 14:12-14 ESV** He said also to the man who had invited him, "When you give a dinner or a banquet, do not invite your friends or your brothers or your relatives or rich neighbors, lest they also invite you in return and you be repaid. (13) But when you give a feast, invite the poor, the crippled, the lame, the blind, (14) and you will be blessed, because they cannot repay you. For you will be repaid at the resurrection of the just."

> **Luke 14:22-24 ESV** And the servant said, 'Sir, what you commanded has been done, and still there is room.' (23) And the master said to the servant, 'Go out to the highways and hedges and compel people to come in, that my house may be filled. (24) For I tell you, none of those men who were invited shall taste my banquet.'"

> **Luke 12:51-53 ESV** Do you think that I have come to give peace on earth? No, I tell you, but rather division. (52) For from now on in one house there will be five divided, three against two and two against three. (53) They will be divided, father against son and son against father, mother against daughter and daughter against mother, mother-in-law against her daughter-in-law and daughter-in-law against mother-in-law."

> *Matthew 10:34-38 ESV "Do not think that I have come to bring peace to the earth. I have not come to bring peace, but a sword. (35) For I have come to set a man against his father, and a daughter against her mother, and a daughter-in-law against her mother-in-law. (36) And a person's enemies will be those of his own household. (37) Whoever loves father or mother more than me is not worthy of me, and whoever loves son or daughter more than me is not worthy of me. (38) And whoever does not take his cross and follow me is not worthy of me.*

It is not the primary intent of our Lord to ensure there is enough meat at the table for the guests to eat. The table has been set and is complete. Our Lord wants to be assured there are enough guests at the invite to fill the spots around the table. The invitation of our Lord is not to be received lightly. We have been invited to a life of being a disciple at the table of our Lord. It is not an easy decision to make a deliberate choice to renounce family for the sake of the Gospel and love for God and His Word. Think about this statement by our Lord in Luke 14:25-26. This Scriptural statement about not loving any family member over the Father was made to Jews. It was an intensely radical statement that went against everything they held to be true culturally and socially concerning family ties. The family was everything! Yet our Lord states that we are not prepared nor fit to be a disciple until we sacrifice all else, including family.

We see in Luke 14 the call of the Lord to come to the feast table and the excuses from the masses as to why they cannot attend. One of the critical statements of Luke 14:18-20 is, **"I must go."** These are the words of many within the Body of Christ today. It would seem that they always have an obligation to go and do something else. They seem to always be under a necessity to attend to the affairs of family and the world yet neglect the matters of Christian discipline, training, and fellowship. I am amazed at how many Christians, especially men, place their job and work over the discipline of following the Father and His demands. They pretend that the affairs of family and the world are so pressing and essential that they cannot find time to attend to their souls. Their family duties or jobs are so demanding they have no time to pray, read the Scriptures, or keep up the worship of God. Even in church services, some Christians allow their cell phones to interfere with fellowship and receiving from the Lord. Are we really so deceived into thinking that our self-importance justifies other things to come between us and uninterrupted time with the Father?

It is amazing the number of people who have made this statement to me, "I wish I had more time to pray and read the Scriptures." It is almost like they are blaming God for being so busy they don't have the time for spiritual matters. Our heavenly Father says that if we first seek God's kingdom and His righteousness, all these things will be added to us. We cannot regard such excuses as family, friends, jobs, and entertainment as legitimate for neglecting our spiritual responsibilities in our walk with God and having fellowship with the saints.

> *Luke 14:18-20 ESV But they all alike began to make excuses. The first said to him, 'I have bought a field, and I must go out and see it. Please have me excused.' (19) And another said, 'I have bought five yoke of oxen, and I go to*

examine them. Please have me excused.' (20) And another said, 'I have married a wife, and therefore I cannot come.'

Matthew 6:33 (ESV) But seek first the kingdom of God and his righteousness, and all these things will be added to you.

Oh, how we need to forsake the ties that bind us, the idols of our own desires we have established, and the pressures that would cause us to compromise our walk with the Lord Jesus Christ. Lord, may we love our families with passionate love, but may it look like hate compared to our love for You.

-5-
TO BE A DISCIPLE OF THE LORD JESUS CHRIST, THERE MUST BE A COMMITMENT TO "DEATH TO SELF" AND TO FOLLOWING CHRIST

Cost #1: Forsake Family Ties
Cost #2: Die To Self

Not only are we called to forsake family ties for the sake of our Lord Jesus Christ, but we are called to die to ourselves. To be a disciple means that all that we have in the areas of time, strength, talents, relationships, gifts, and our own lives will be demanded as a sacrifice to the Lord for His glory. We are called to the cross. We are called to be among the tribe of the "crucified ones."

> **Romans 12:1-2 ESV I appeal to you therefore, brothers, by the mercies of God, to present your bodies as a living sacrifice, holy and acceptable to God, which is your spiritual worship. (2) Do not be conformed to this world, but be transformed by the renewal of your mind, that by testing you may discern what is the will of God, what is good and acceptable and perfect.**
>
> **1 Peter 2:4-5 ESV As you come to him, a living stone rejected by men but in the sight of God chosen and precious, (5) you yourselves like living stones are being built up as a spiritual house, to be a holy priesthood, to offer spiritual**

> *sacrifices acceptable to God through Jesus Christ.*
>
> **Romans 6:6 ESV** *We know that our old self was crucified with him in order that the body of sin might be brought to nothing, so that we would no longer be enslaved to sin.*
>
> **Galatians 2:20 ESV** *I have been crucified with Christ. It is no longer I who live, but Christ who lives in me. And the life I now live in the flesh I live by faith in the Son of God, who loved me and gave himself for me.*

The sacrifice demanded in Romans 12:1 must be holy and acceptable to God, meaning He is not obligated to accept whatever we bring, including our left-over time. He requires the first fruits of our lives. Becoming a disciple is a daily walk and lifetime of yielding our lives in order to become formed into the likeness of our Lord. In our self-centered nature, this is not possible. It takes a daily decision to die to our will and ways and to follow the Lord Jesus Christ.

> **Luke 14:27 ESV** *Whoever does not bear his own cross and come after me cannot be my disciple.*

In the first century, when a person was condemned to be crucified, a part of the sentence was that he should carry the cross on which he was to die to his place of execution. We find that our Lord carried his cross through the most populated part of the city until he fainted from fatigue, exhaustion, and pain. To carry the cross to the place of execution was an incredible added burden that was disgraceful and extremely emotional. Bearing the cross was an addition to the punishment which had already been inflicted through the trial and beatings. To bear one's cross was an admission of guilt and submission to the authority and laws of the one executing judgment. In the Gospels, when the mandate "to carry the cross" is used, we know that it is a figurative expression, showing that we must endure whatever burden, emotional trial, or disgrace in following our Lord Jesus Christ. Part of our duties as disciples is to let the people of the world think or speak of us as they may and us doing what is required within the Scriptures, even if it produces shame, disgrace, or pain to our soulish man.

When we die to ourselves, we also die to all we have and our desires and wants. The best way to do this is to choose to live a life that leaves the attitude of ownership and move into management or stewardship of all that we have. That way, we declare all that we have, including our body, as belonging to the Lord. In everything, we are called to be faithful stewards.

Luke 14:33 ESV So therefore, any one of you who does not renounce all that he has cannot be my disciple.

I sang an old hymn for years and years called "I Surrender All." In my early years of singing that song, I felt like a hypocrite knowing that I was not willing to surrender all to the Lord.

It is amazing that as years go by and we grow in the Lord, the things we thought we could not do without now seem to be a burden. When we fail to give ourselves, our wants, our desires, and our possessions to the Lord, we will fail to distinguish between what we really need versus what we just want. When we fail to yield ourselves up, we also fail to recognize the vast difference between the temporal kingdoms of this world versus the eternal kingdom of God. So here we are with the typical Christian home filled with stuff in addition to storage sheds filled with our overflow. To repeat an old saying that still echoes truth, "Our Lord Jesus Christ must be Lord of all, or He is not Lord at all."

> *Matthew 16:24-27 ESV Then Jesus told his disciples, "If anyone would come after me, let him deny himself and take up his cross and follow me. (25) For whoever would save his life will lose it, but whoever loses his life for my sake will find it. (26) For what will it profit a man if he gains the whole world and forfeits his soul? Or what shall a man give in return for his soul? (27) For the Son of Man is going to come with his angels in the glory of his Father, and then he will repay each person according to what he has done.*
>
> *Luke 17:33 ESV Whoever seeks to preserve his life will lose it, but whoever loses his life will keep it.*

Imagine if we really understood the call and the cost of being a disciple of the Lord Jesus Christ. If we truly understood the price, we would not try to explain away Scriptures like "let the dead bury the dead" as just a first-century mandate of a different culture or society. In true discipleship, we would know and understand the importance of following the Lord in a "suddenly moment" like the disciples did when they *IMMEDIATELY* left all to follow the Lord.

> *Matthew 4:21-22 ESV And going on from there he saw two other brothers, James the son of Zebedee and John his brother, in the boat with*

Zebedee their father, mending their nets, and he called them. (22) Immediately they left the boat and their father and followed him.

Luke 9:57-62 ESV As they were going along the road, someone said to him, "I will follow you wherever you go." (58) And Jesus said to him, "Foxes have holes, and birds of the air have nests, but the Son of Man has nowhere to lay his head." (59) To another he said, "Follow me." But he said, "Lord, let me first go and bury my father." (60) And Jesus said to him, "Leave the dead to bury their own dead. But as for you, go and proclaim the kingdom of God." (61) Yet another said, "I will follow you, Lord, but let me first say farewell to those at my home." (62) Jesus said to him, "No one who puts his hand to the plow and looks back is fit for the kingdom of God."

Being a disciple of our Lord Jesus Christ is not made in a five-minute heated emotional decision and then nothing of substance afterward. It is a lifestyle of denying self and cross-bearing. The cross is not a burden imposed upon a believer. The cross is something a believer desiring to be a disciple willingly chooses for the sake of the Gospel message.

At the believers' cross of dying to self, God will become first in all things: over family, friends, finances, and fun. Before any believer chooses the life of discipleship, he is first called upon to *"COUNT THE COST."* The mandate of "forsaking all" in order to be a disciple is not an option. The Lord makes it clear if we do not forsake all, we cannot be a disciple. This requirement is a "fly in the face" command when we weigh it against our free enterprise society that says

:
- "Get all that you can get"
- "Be all you can be"
- "Have it your way"
- "You deserve a break today."

In the Bible, God's economy says, "die or be killed." We cannot become a disciple our way any more than we can have salvation our way. It is all God's plan; many are called, but few are chosen.

> *Luke 20:18 ESV Everyone who falls on that stone will be broken to pieces, and when it falls on anyone, it will crush him."*
>
> *Luke 14:25-33 ESV Now great crowds accompanied him, and he turned and said to them, (26) "If anyone comes to me and does not hate his own father and mother and wife and children and brothers and sisters, yes, and even his own life, he cannot be my disciple. (27) Whoever does not bear his own cross and come after me cannot be my disciple. (28) For which of you, desiring to build a tower, does not first sit down and count the cost, whether he has enough to complete it? (29) Otherwise, when he has laid a foundation and is not able to finish, all who see it begin to mock him, (30) saying, 'This man began to build and was not able to finish.' (31) Or what king, going out to encounter another king in war, will not sit down first and deliberate whether he is able with ten thousand to meet him who comes against him with twenty thousand? (32) And if not, while the other is yet a great way off, he sends a delegation and asks for terms of peace.*

THE COST OF DISCIPLESHIP

(33) *So therefore, any one of you who does not renounce all that he has cannot be my disciple.*

Being made a genuine Biblical disciple includes careful planning and sacrifice. In Luke 14:28-30, a man who decided to build a tower counted the cost first to ensure he could complete it. In Luke 14:31-32, a king who decided to go into battle first agreed if he had enough men to fight and win. These examples show us that we need to count the cost before choosing to be a disciple of our Lord. This evaluation is an act of loyalty to our Lord through our commitment to give up everything, even our lives. This requirement is not an option in order to be a disciple of the Lord Jesus Christ. It is not one of those things where we can go ahead and get our certificate and promise to fulfill the classroom training later. We *CANNOT* be a disciple of our Lord *until all is forsaken* and we are dead to ourselves! It takes Christ living in us to live a true victorious Christian life.

There is an old saying to help us identify with the teaching of Luke 14:33. "If I own something that I cannot live without and I cannot give away, then I really don't own it. It owns me." I had to remember this over the last few years as I started giving my guitars away. I have been playing the guitar since I was thirteen years old. My musical talent has been a source of both entertainment and a source of giving praise to the Father. Dying to self also means devaluing the things that are tied to self. When this passage says to "forsake all," it is more than items or something we have in our possession. Often, possessions have deep emotional or mental ties assigned to them, such as my music and musical instruments.

Dying to self includes dying to family, friends, birthplace, and even our name. It becomes more convenient to part with a possession that has lost its emotional and mental hold. It was like the Abrahamic Covenant of Genesis 12:1-3 when God gave Abraham a new land, a new people, and a new name.

To be a true Biblical disciple is to walk away from all that identifies us as who we are in exchange for all that identifies Christ and who He is in us. Wow! It is a life of suffering for His sake because we are perfected in suffering.

If we see the connection of Luke 14 to the cross of our Lord, we know He was speaking and teaching prophetically concerning His death. He gave all and forsook all for the greater good, which is giving the Father glory and redeeming mankind. At this point, the disciples did not realize our Lord Jesus Christ was laying His life on the cross for their sins so that they could have life. In this, we see that being a disciple, although a Biblical mandate, is not for the faint of heart.

We see that Luke 14 finished the discussion of becoming a disciple by using the example of salt. It is funny how many times Luke 14:34-35 has been preached without mentioning the rest of Luke chapter 14 and the topic of discipleship. But the illustrations in Luke 14 concerning discipleship must include the example of being salt.

Salt is valuable. Salt is not valuable because of its color because many things are white. Salt is not valuable because of its texture because many things are granulated. The distinctive qualities of salt are its taste which is its seasoning ability, its ability to preserve, and its ability to create thirst.

These are all traits of being an authentic disciple of our Lord. If salt loses these qualities, then it is worthless and is no longer worthy of being called "salt." A lack of commitment to our Lord Jesus Christ as a disciple is like salt without flavor, without preservative power, and without the ability to create thirst. Can you imagine the example of our Lord when He said that when salt has lost the three qualities that make it salt, it is not even worth the dunghill?

> **Luke 14:34-35 ESV "Salt is good, but if salt has lost its taste, how shall its saltiness be restored? (35) It is of no use either for the soil or for the manure pile. It is thrown away. He who has ears to hear, let him hear."**

We should embrace the life of being a disciple by forsaking any family ties that exalt itself over our love for our Lord Jesus Christ, and we should live a life of death, of bearing the cross, and of self-sacrifice that He might be exalted. Remember that the life we live is the resurrected Lord in and through us. We must allow Christ to live His life through us.

> **Galatians 2:20 (ESV) I have been crucified with Christ. It is no longer I who live, but Christ who lives in me. And the life I now live in the flesh I live by faith in the Son of God, who loved me and gave himself for me.**

-6-
TO BE A DISCIPLE OF THE LORD JESUS CHRIST, THERE MUST BE A COMMITMENT TOWARD FAITHFULNESS

Cost #1: Forsake Family Ties
Cost #2: Die To Self
Cost #3: Walk In Faithfulness

We know by now that we are called to be a disciple. In being a disciple, we have seen that we are called to forsake family ties that are exalted over our love for our Lord. We are also called to forsake our own life and realize our salvation is a life exchange. We gave the Lord our broken lives, and He gave us His life. The third area of being a disciple is learning to walk in faithfulness. We all know someone who is double-minded, flighty, and unfaithful to their promises. These people speak a lot and promise much but seldom come through. When they talk, it is empty words like a cloud without water. If we were ever in a crisis situation, these unfaithful, double-minded Christians are not the ones which we would want to place our life and trust into.

We want to know that someone is dependable. This type of reputation is true with our spouses, children, the people who build our homes, fix our cars, and our doctors. But it is especially true for those who stand in ministry with us. Only faithful (true and sure) people are reliable to be qualified for discipleship training. What is faithfulness? Faithful means a person is "full of faith, trustworthy, dependable, and believable." It is only natural for us to desire to know trustworthy, dependable, and believable people.

These character traits seemed commonplace when I was a child walking around with my grandfather, Mr. Ernest Dewey Downey, in Virginia. I watched him enter into contracts with people with a word and handshake and standing solid like concrete only upon the word of an honest man. I watched that trait slip away from society as I grew older. I saw that a man's word or handshake could no longer be trusted. In fact, it seldom meant much when people entered an agreement by signing legal documents. The Scriptures say that men are liars, but God is true.

> **Romans 3:4 ESV By no means! Let God be true though every one were a liar, as it is written, "That you may be justified in your words, and prevail when you are judged."**

May we carry the character of our heavenly Father and be faithful people that can be depended upon, whereby our word is our bond.

> **Numbers 23:19-20 ESV God is not man, that he should lie, or a son of man, that he should change his mind. Has he said, and will he not do it? Or has he spoken, and will he not fulfill it? (20) Behold, I received a command to bless: he has blessed, and I cannot revoke it.**

> **2 Peter 3:9 ESV The Lord is not slow to fulfill his promise as some count slowness, but is patient toward you, not wishing that any should perish, but that all should reach repentance.**

I remember going into specialty shops that sold very expensive Fine China. There were signs everywhere asking people not to touch the merchandise. There were signs everywhere saying, "You break it, you buy it." It was a reminder by the store owner that the contents of the establishment were of great value and those "just looking" should be careful. This example is an excellent picture concerning the precious things of my Lord Jesus Christ that He has entrusted to my care. Being faithful is being dependable, trustworthy, true, and believable. However, being faithful also means to "handle with care."

I have moved across the USA and Germany many times, and most of those times, I packed my belongings and moved myself. With each move, I can hear Debby, my wife, at some point saying, "Be careful. I trust that you packed those things correctly." She was counting on my faithfulness to do the right thing in handling her possessions. Likewise, I know that I am called to be a faithful steward of the gifting, the talents, the possessions, and the callings which the Lord has entrusted to my oversight. I hear His call, "Be careful, and be found faithful." For all the Elders or Pastors in ministry, I want to say that we are to be careful and be found faithful stewards of the precious lives and the Word of God that the Father has placed in our hands.

> ***1 Corinthians 4:1-2 ESV (1) This is how one should regard us, as servants of Christ and stewards of the mysteries of God. (2) Moreover, it is required of stewards that they be found faithful.***
>
> ***Luke 12:41-44 ESV Peter said, "Lord, are you telling this parable for us or for all?" (42) And the Lord said, "Who then is the faithful and wise***

> *manager, whom his master will set over his household, to give them their portion of food at the proper time? (43) Blessed is that servant whom his master will find so doing when he comes. (44) Truly, I say to you, he will set him over all his possessions.*

The Lord is looking for the faithful man who will teach a faithful man who, in turn, will teach a faithful man. The Apostle Paul was a faithful man. Paul instructed Timothy, who was a faithful man. Paul told Timothy to teach faithful men who will teach faithful men. I do not like to use my time on people who do not have ears to hear and just want to operate as time stealers.

> *2 Timothy 2:1-4 ESV You then, my child, be strengthened by the grace that is in Christ Jesus, (2) and what you have heard from me in the presence of many witnesses entrust to faithful men who will be able to teach others also. (3) Share in suffering as a good soldier of Christ Jesus. (4) No soldier gets entangled in civilian pursuits, since his aim is to please the one who enlisted him.*

It is evident from the Scriptures that being faithful is a major priority with our Lord. Sadly, faithfulness is a trait that is so lacking within the body of Christ. This void reveals the need for believers to earnestly desire to become disciples. The Scriptures teach if we are faithful in small things, we will get larger things, and if we are faithful in that which belongs to another man, we will receive our own.

If we are going to be good godly stewards, then we need to be found faithful which is one of the requirements or pieces of evidence of being a disciple. We are to be faithful both in our field and in another man's field. We must be faithful in a little if we expect to receive a lot.

> **Luke 16:10-12 ESV** "One who is faithful in a very little is also faithful in much, and one who is dishonest in a very little is also dishonest in much. (11) If then you have not been faithful in the unrighteous wealth, who will entrust to you the true riches? (12) And if you have not been faithful in that which is another's, who will give you that which is your own?**
>
> **1 Corinthians 4:1-2 ESV (1)** This is how one should regard us, as servants of Christ and stewards of the mysteries of God. **(2)** Moreover, it is required of stewards that they be found faithful.
>
> **Matthew 25:21-23 ESV** His master said to him, 'Well done, good and faithful servant. You have been faithful over a little; I will set you over much. Enter into the joy of your master.' **(22)** And he also who had the two talents came forward, saying, 'Master, you delivered to me two talents; here I have made two talents more.' **(23)** His master said to him, 'Well done, good and faithful servant. You have been faithful over a little; I will set you over much. Enter into the joy of your master.'

There was such a commitment to giving up everything among the early disciples they even confessed they had nothing to return to. We need a dose of this kind of discipleship among the body of Christ today. Imagine this for a moment: The commitment to being a disciple is so intense in our life in reality and not in theory that we could say, "Lord, where would I go if I turned back?" Homes gone! Land gone! Family gone! All for the sake of the Gospel, which is the good news! Just because we are called to sacrifice all for Christ does not make the good news bad news.

When we think about being a disciple, we find many Scriptures that teach us to withdraw from ownership and enter into management or stewardship. Since we have been bought with a price and no longer belong to ourselves, it would stand to reason all that we own needs to be turned over to the Lord, and we take on the servant role of stewards of it. The disciples found making choices difficult as they gave up everything for the Gospel of our Lord. The disciples wanted to know what to expect as their reward for their commitment and sacrifice of faithfulness. They had left their jobs, homes, and families to follow the Lord. With the high cost of true Biblical discipleship, our Lord ended up with just a handful of the faithful who turned the world upside down (or right side up). However, not everyone embraced this lifestyle of discipleship, and many turned away from the Lord and walked no more with Him.

> **Mark 10:28-31 ESV Peter began to say to him, "See, we have left everything and followed you." (29) Jesus said, "Truly, I say to you, there is no one who has left house or brothers or sisters or mother or father or children or lands, for my sake and for the gospel, (30) who will not receive a hundredfold now in this time, houses and brothers and sisters and mothers and children and lands, with persecutions, and in the age to come eternal life. (31) But many who are first will be last, and the last first."**

John 6:63-69 ESV It is the Spirit who gives life; the flesh is no help at all. The words that I have spoken to you are spirit and life. (64) But there are some of you who do not believe." (For Jesus knew from the beginning who those were who did not believe, and who it was who would betray him.) (65) And he said, "This is why I told you that no one can come to me unless it is granted him by the Father." (66) After this many of his disciples turned back and no longer walked with him. (67) So Jesus said to the Twelve, "Do you want to go away as well?" (68) Simon Peter answered him, "Lord, to whom shall we go? You have the words of eternal life, (69) and we have believed, and have come to know, that you are the Holy One of God."

Can you hear Simon Peter asking our Lord, "Where or to whom shall we go?" What a great question. Yet because of peer and family pressure, many believers return to where they had previously been delivered. A short statement in the Scriptures should keep us focused on the cost of turning our face towards Christ and then being tempted to turn away. It is the second shortest verse in the Bible, yet it carries volumes of information.

Luke 17:32 ESV Remember Lot's wife.

Luke 16:10-12 ESV "One who is faithful in a very little is also faithful in much, and one who is dishonest in a very little is also dishonest in much. (11) If then you have not been faithful in the unrighteous wealth, who will entrust to you the true riches? (12) And if you have not been faithful in that which is another's, who will give you that which is your own?

Luke 19:16-17 ESV The first came before him, saying, 'Lord, your mina has made ten minas more.' (17) And he said to him, 'Well done, good servant! Because you have been faithful in a very little, you shall have authority over ten cities.'

The Word of God teaches that being faithful carries some promises. When someone does not act in the way of being faithful, then the opposite is true. This teaching means the person is double-minded and unstable instead of being trustworthy, dependable, and believable. The Word of God promises that the unfaithful or double-minded man will receive nothing from the Lord.

James 1:6-8 ESV But let him ask in faith, with no doubting, for the one who doubts is like a wave of the sea that is driven and tossed by the wind. (7) For that person must not suppose that he will receive anything from the Lord; (8) he is a double-minded man, unstable in all his ways.

If we choose to become disciples, we need to know that we can trust our mentors. Our first line of authority as our spiritual mentor is the Lord Jesus Christ. He can be completely trusted in all things and all areas of our life. The next thing we need to trust is the Word of God. The Word is pure and righteous and can be trusted in all life situations.

Proverbs 30:5-6 ESV Every word of God proves true; he is a shield to those who take refuge in him. (6) Do not add to his words, lest he rebuke you and you be found a liar.

Psalms 18:30-36 ESV This God—his way is perfect; the word of the LORD proves true; he is a shield for all those who take refuge in him. (31) For who is God, but the LORD? And who is a rock, except our God?— (32) the God who equipped me with strength and made my way blameless. (33) He made my feet like the feet of a deer and set me secure on the heights. (34) He trains my hands for war, so that my arms can bend a bow of bronze. (35) You have given me the shield of your salvation, and your right hand supported me, and your gentleness made me great. (36) You gave a wide place for my steps under me, and my feet did not slip.

Embracing the life of a disciple means embracing a life where we do not exalt family ties over our love for our Lord, living a life of denying self, and walking in faithfulness.

-7-
TO BE A DISCIPLE OF THE LORD JESUS CHRIST, THERE MUST BE A COMMITMENT TOWARDS LOVING THE LORD JESUS CHRIST AND LOVING ONE ANOTHER

Cost #1: Forsake Family Ties
Cost #2: Die To Self
Cost #3: Walk In Faithfulness
Cost #4: Love God And Others

As we learn the disciplines of exalting our Lord over all family relationships, the way of the cross and self-sacrifice, and the daily commitment to being faithful, we internalize truths on our way to becoming a disciple of our Lord. The fourth trait of being a disciple is properly loving God and loving one another. Let it be stated that love is a deliberate choice and an action, unlike the misconception that it is only an emotion.

There are 1,050 commands in the New Testament. Some are commands concerning the things we are NOT to do. Some are commands relating to the things we ARE to do. We know that as believers, we are to love one another. Yet, the Word commands us in many Scriptures to love one another. Why do we need the commands to love? Because it is easier not to love people in our flesh, the Father had to remind us of His Word by commanding us to love.

We might believe in our mind that love is a choice, but by action and confession, many believers still see love as an emotion. That is why we use the terms "fall in love" or "fell out of love." If love is strictly emotional, we can fall in and out of love based on how we feel. But love is both a choice and an action. It is something of the will and something we do. This doctrinal reality is why the Church of Ephesus in Revelation 2:1-5 was rebuked for leaving their first love. It was their action based on choice.

> **Revelation 2:4-5 ESV But I have this against you, that you have abandoned the love you had at first. (5) Remember therefore from where you have fallen; repent, and do the works you did at first. If not, I will come to you and remove your lampstand from its place, unless you repent.**

We are commanded to love because we decide to do it out of our will and not based on how we feel. When we read John 13:34-35, we should be grieved because of the lack of love towards one another within the body of Christ.

> **John 13:34-35 ESV A new commandment I give to you, that you love one another: just as I have loved you, you also are to love one another. (35) By this all people will know that you are my disciples, if you have love for one another."**

When our Lord gave us this command to love, He also gave the world the right to judge us by our love. Many times we may see tolerance, worldly friendship, romance, and common sports or activities, among believers, and we may see social gatherings and meals among believers. However, do we know a lot of believers who really love one another with God's unconditional love? This unconditional agape love attracts lost people to the heart of God and reveals that we are disciples of our Lord Jesus Christ.

The type of love we receive from the Father and give to the people is given in John 13:34. We are to love others as the Lord loved us. This love has no room for selfishness, rejection, rebellion, fear, envy, strife, and jealousy. A deep love relationship with God and others is not just a confession of the mouth but a life proven through daily obedience. Many say they love the Lord Jesus Christ but then live a life of selfishness filled with the wants and desires of the world.

> **Matthew 15:8-9 ESV** "'This people honors me with their lips, but their heart is far from me; (9) in vain do they worship me, teaching as doctrines the commandments of men.'"

Our Lord Jesus speaks about those who say they love Him versus being a disciple and obeying Him out of a deep love relationship. Remember this thought taken from 1 John 4:19: "It takes God to love God!"

> **1 John 4:19 ESV** We love because he first loved us.

The only reason or way we can love God is to receive His love and then return it. The disciple of God is committed to God's Word and fellowship with the Father in conversation (known as prayer) and cultivating a deep love relationship. Love towards God and others must be in word, deed, and thought.

> **Colossians 3:17 ESV** And whatever you do, in word or deed, do everything in the name of the

Lord Jesus, giving thanks to God the Father through him.

1 John 4:6-8 ESV We are from God. Whoever knows God listens to us; whoever is not from God does not listen to us. By this we know the Spirit of truth and the spirit of error. (7) Beloved, let us love one another, for love is from God, and whoever loves has been born of God and knows God. (8) Anyone who does not love does not know God, because God is love.

1 John 4:15-16 ESV Whoever confesses that Jesus is the Son of God, God abides in him, and he in God. (16) So we have come to know and to believe the love that God has for us. God is love, and whoever abides in love abides in God, and God abides in him.

1 John 4:18-21 ESV There is no fear in love, but perfect love casts out fear. For fear has to do with punishment, and whoever fears has not been perfected in love. (19) We love because he first loved us. (20) If anyone says, "I love God," and hates his brother, he is a liar; for he who does not love his brother whom he has seen cannot love God whom he has not seen. (21) And this commandment we have from him: whoever loves God must also love his brother.

We live in a day where both non-believers and believers do what is right in their own eyes. When many of us hear that statement, we think the believer must be out in the world doing some grossly immoral thing. But "doing what is right in one's own eyes" carries more than outward sin. It is an attitude of the selfishness of the heart. It is a state of feeling comfortable in our own abilities and intellect, even when it is causing discomfort in those around us and negatively affecting the atmosphere. I don't want to sound like "new age" with that comment, so let me state it this way. We have heard the statement, "who is going to address the elephant in the room?" When we walk in our own way, we leave an atmosphere of unrest, heaviness, anger, or hostility, among others. People walk on eggshells around us because they fear speaking their minds and upsetting the apple cart. This atmosphere is far from the love relationship our Lord taught us.

Example: Many of us experienced times sitting in a room waiting for the Bible study to begin, and then the teacher comes in, and there is a complete atmosphere change in the room. He walks in with the authority, the anointing, and the love of God on him, and immediately the people prepare themselves to hear what the man of God has to say. It is an honor given to him because of his love relationship with the Lord and towards the people. There is an atmosphere of peace and anticipation that he will take them to the heart of the Father.

> *John 13:34-35 ESV A new commandment I give to you, that you love one another: just as I have loved you, you also are to love one another. (35) By this all people will know that you are my disciples, if you have love for one another."*

> *Ephesians 3:14-21 ESV For this reason I bow my knees before the Father, (15) from whom every family in heaven and on earth is named, (16) that according to the riches of his glory he may grant you to be strengthened with power through his Spirit in your inner being, (17) so that Christ may*

> *dwell in your hearts through faith—that you, being rooted and grounded in love, (18) may have strength to comprehend with all the saints what is the breadth and length and height and depth, (19) and to know the love of Christ that surpasses knowledge, that you may be filled with all the fullness of God. (20) Now to him who is able to do far more abundantly than all that we ask or think, according to the power at work within us, (21) to him be glory in the church and in Christ Jesus throughout all generations, forever and ever. Amen.*

Example Continued: The following week, a different speaker or teacher comes into the room, and the atmosphere changes but this time in the negative. The people are unsettled and without peace and find it hard to give their attention to the speaker. He may be as good of a teacher as the first, but he has a different spirit. He seems to teach them just to hear his voice or to complete a task, yet the people do not see the love of God or sense that he loves them. We need to walk in a way that displays the love of God in our lives. We must walk out His will and not be guilty of doing what is right in our own eyes. People need to know that we love them. This decision to love does not mean we are to compromise truth for the doctrines of man, creeds, codes, or false religious activities. Just because someone is offended and reacts to our teaching does not mean our love for them decreases. It just means they have blocked receiving the love of God or our love because they are dull of hearing due to an offended heart.

> *Matthew 6:33 ESV But seek first the kingdom of God and his righteousness, and all these things will be added to you.*

THE COST OF DISCIPLESHIP

Seeking the Kingdom of God always starts with loving God with all of heart, soul, mind, and strength and seeking Him and His righteousness. So, as we choose to become a disciple of Christ, we learn to forsake all relationships that are exalted over our Lord, deny ourselves and learn the way of the cross, be faithful in small things and another man's field, and walk in a love relationship with God and with others.

-8-
TO BE A DISCIPLE OF THE LORD JESUS CHRIST, THERE MUST BE A COMMITMENT TOWARD SPIRITUAL HUNGER AND THIRST

Cost #1: Forsake Family Ties
Cost #2: Die To Self
Cost #3: Walk In Faithfulness
Cost #4: Love God And Others
Cost #5: A Spiritual Hunger And Thirst

The commitment to being a disciple is not so easy to walk out. If walking out discipleship was easy, everyone in the church would be doing it. We can become mentally and emotionally overwhelmed when we think about exalting Christ over all family ties and relationships and then dying to ourselves and our wants. We are called to be faithful in all our ways in word, deed, and thought. We are also called to love God with all our heart, soul, mind, and strength and to love others as we love ourselves.

> **Romans 14:17-18 ESV For the kingdom of God is not a matter of eating and drinking but of righteousness and peace and joy in the Holy Spirit. (18) Whoever thus serves Christ is acceptable to God and approved by men.**
>
> **Matthew 5:6 ESV "Blessed are those who hunger and thirst for righteousness, for they shall be satisfied.**

THE COST OF DISCIPLESHIP

The fifth trait of becoming a disciple of our Lord Jesus Christ is having a hunger and thirst for spiritual things. Someone who desires to be a disciple has deep spiritual hunger and thirst to grow and be used by God to advance the Kingdom. There have been a lot of songs over the last twenty years concerning thirst. It is imperative for a believer to get and stay hungry and thirsty for the things of God if the believer is to become a disciple of our Lord. I see a lot of hunger in the body of Christ. However, it is not always directed toward God. I see a desire for signs and wonders, entertainment, promotion, and popularity among believers. We have the promise that if we hunger and thirst for righteousness, we will be filled.

What has happened is that many have departmentalized their spiritual lives. In the corporate church, there is a cry for God to satisfy their hunger and thirst for righteousness and the fulfillment of kingdom truths and promises. But outside the corporate fellowship, the believer can quickly be influenced and fall into the world's trap. Then his flesh seeks to satisfy the hunger and thirst for more things of the world. Then, at their vocation, there is the trap of falling into the hunger and thirst for worldly success. But for the one who truly desires to be a disciple of the Lord Jesus Christ, the Christian life is the same no matter the setting.

> **Psalms 107:9 ESV For he satisfies the longing soul, and the hungry soul he fills with good things.**
>
> **Luke 1:53 ESV he has filled the hungry with good things, and the rich he has sent away empty.**

Luke 6:20-21 ESV And he lifted up his eyes on his disciples, and said: "Blessed are you who are poor, for yours is the kingdom of God. (21) "Blessed are you who are hungry now, for you shall be satisfied. "Blessed are you who weep now, for you shall laugh.

Isaiah 55:1-2 ESV "Come, everyone who thirsts, come to the waters; and he who has no money, come, buy and eat! Come, buy wine and milk without money and without price. (2) Why do you spend your money for that which is not bread, and your labor for that which does not satisfy? Listen diligently to me, and eat what is good, and delight yourselves in rich food.

John 4:14 ESV but whoever drinks of the water that I will give him will never be thirsty again. The water that I will give him will become in him a spring of water welling up to eternal life."

John 7:37-38 ESV On the last day of the feast, the great day, Jesus stood up and cried out, "If anyone thirsts, let him come to me and drink. (38) Whoever believes in me, as the Scripture has said, 'Out of his heart will flow rivers of living water.'"

There should be no departmentalization of social life versus vocational life versus spiritual life versus family life. There should be a commitment to hunger and thirst for God and His righteousness in all areas of life.

Matthew 4:4 ESV But he answered, "It is written, "'Man shall not live by bread alone, but by every word that comes from the mouth of God.'"

THE COST OF DISCIPLESHIP

The Greek meaning for "word" in Matthew 4:4 is "Rhema" and is the "spoken word, or the word uttered, narrated, commanded or disputed." God is calling us to be at a place of thirst that is more than physical. Our soul, which is our thoughts or mind, our emotions or feelings, and our will or choices, should deeply long for the heart of God. The disciple realizes that his next breath is because of the Lord. The true disciple does not desire the world and worldly things but longs to be before the presence of the Father.

> **Acts 17:28 ESV** *for "'In him we live and move and have our being'; as even some of your own poets have said, "'For we are indeed his offspring.'*
>
> **Psalms 42:1-4 ESV** *To the choirmaster. A Maskil of the Sons of Korah. As a deer pants for flowing streams, so pants my soul for you, O God. (2) My soul thirsts for God, for the living God. When shall I come and appear before God? (3) My tears have been my food day and night, while they say to me all the day long, "Where is your God?" (4) These things I remember, as I pour out my soul: how I would go with the throng and lead them in procession to the house of God with glad shouts and songs of praise, a multitude keeping festival.*
>
> **1 Chronicles 16:8-12 ESV** *(8) Oh give thanks to the LORD; call upon his name; make known his deeds among the peoples! (9) Sing to him, sing praises to him; tell of all his wondrous works! (10) Glory in his holy name; let the hearts of those who seek the LORD rejoice! (11) Seek the LORD and his strength; seek his presence*

continually! (12) Remember the wondrous works that he has done, his miracles and the judgments he uttered,

Psalms 63:1-4 ESV A Psalm of David, when he was in the wilderness of Judah. O God, you are my God; earnestly I seek you; my soul thirsts for you; my flesh faints for you, as in a dry and weary land where there is no water. (2) So I have looked upon you in the sanctuary, beholding your power and glory. (3) Because your steadfast love is better than life, my lips will praise you. (4) So I will bless you as long as I live; in your name I will lift up my hands.

Spiritual hunger and thirst mean that, as best as we know, we live a cleansed life and are passionate about deep fellowship with the heavenly Father. Being spiritually hungry implies that at any cost, we will position ourselves to be able to sit at the table of the Lord. In our spiritual journey to become disciples of the Lord, we must keep our "confession lists" small and up to date. This statement means that our confession of sin need not be only on a Sunday during an invitation call. God wants to bless our lives and will do so in a life that is "confessed-up-to-date." According to the Bible, there are two kinds of Christians, the spiritual and the carnal or sensual, which I call the believing believers (the spiritual) and the unbelieving believers (the carnal). This can also be referred to as those who walk in the Spirit surrendering to God's will versus those who walk according to the deeds of the flesh.

Galatians 5:16 ESV But I say, walk by the Spirit, and you will not gratify the desires of the flesh.

THE COST OF DISCIPLESHIP

> **1 Corinthians 3:1-3 ESV (1) But I, brothers, could not address you as spiritual people, but as people of the flesh, as infants in Christ. (2) I fed you with milk, not solid food, for you were not ready for it. And even now you are not yet ready, (3) for you are still of the flesh. For while there is jealousy and strife among you, are you not of the flesh and behaving only in a human way?**

The carnal Christian hungers and thirsts also, but it is for attention, for what other people have, and for their own selfish ways. Spiritual believers are those who walk in the Spirit and yield up their desires and hunger for the desires of God. There are two kinds of spiritual Christians. The first are those who are disciples and are either mentoring others or desiring to mentor others. The second are those who want to be disciples and are hungering and thirsting for spiritual growth and seeking someone to mentor them in the things of the Kingdom.

> **Galatians 6:1-3 ESV Brothers, if anyone is caught in any transgression, you who are spiritual should restore him in a spirit of gentleness. Keep watch on yourself, lest you too be tempted. (2) Bear one another's burdens, and so fulfill the law of Christ. (3) For if anyone thinks he is something, when he is nothing, he deceives himself.**

> **Ephesians 4:32 ESV Be kind to one another, tenderhearted, forgiving one another, as God in Christ forgave you.**

Being a disciple costs us everything. We have covered five Biblical costs of being a disciple up to this point.

1. We must forsake all family relationships for the relationship of knowing Christ.
2. We must die to ourselves and live the life of the cross.
3. We must be faithful in word, deed, and thought.
4. We must love God and others with unconditional love.
5. In all this, we must develop a passionate hunger and thirst for God and His righteousness. None of these demands are easy, but we have Biblical assurance that we can do all things through Christ Jesus, who strengthens us. God would not call us to something we could not do in and through Him.

THE COST OF DISCIPLESHIP

-9-
TO BE A DISCIPLE OF THE LORD JESUS CHRIST, THERE MUST BE A COMMITMENT TO HAVING A TEACHABLE ATTITUDE

Cost #1: Forsake Family Ties
Cost #2: Die To Self
Cost #3: Walk In Faithfulness
Cost #4: Love God And Others
Cost #5: A Spiritual Hunger And Thirst
Cost #6: Being Teachable

HAVING EARS TO HEAR

Being teachable is the sixth trait of becoming a disciple of our Lord Jesus Christ. To be teachable means having ears to hear. To be teachable also means we learn to abide in the Word of God. Abiding in the Word is like getting married. It is relatively easy to go through the marriage ceremony, but there is much more to the marriage than the ceremony. Marriage after the ceremony is a dedicated daily commitment to build a continuing relationship. We can read the Bible from cover to cover like it is our marriage ceremony, but to abide in the Word and to have the Word abide in us, we need commitment and a continuing relationship. To use a phrase my brother Pastor Andrew Crawley always says, "We are married to the truth."

We should not misuse or misquote Scriptures and recognize the misuse when others do so. Some of the

Scriptures that are commonly misused are John 8:31-32. If we call ourselves a disciple of the Lord, then we need to be a person of the Word.

> **John 8:31-32 ESV So Jesus said to the Jews who had believed him, "If you abide in my word, you are truly my disciples, (32) and you will know the truth, and the truth will set you free."**

Believers run around quoting John 8:32 like it has "magic power" to change them and set them free. But using John 8:32 that way is pulling a Scripture out of context and misusing it. It is trying to make "microwave popcorn" Christianity. We want a lot, and we want it fast. It is the "Lord, I want patience, and I want it now" syndrome. The teaching of John 8:32 must remain in connection with verse 31 and the complete chapter of John 8. The key of John 8:31-32 is the word "continue" in verse 31. The Greek word for continue is "meno" and means to "give place to, abide, dwell, endure, be present with, remain, stand, and tarry." These words should help us to see that being a disciple is not reading or quoting a Scripture once in a while when convenient.

Why do we read the Scriptures? Is it just to fill our heads with knowledge and facts so we can communicate intellectually with others with the appearance of being spiritual? The real purpose of us abiding in the Word and having the Word abiding in us should be to grow in faith, have our lives changed into the likeness of Christ, and glorify and honor the Father. In John 15:7-8 we find another Scripture often taken out of context and misused.

> **John 15:7-8 ESV If you abide in me, and my words abide in you, ask whatever you wish, and it**

> **will be done for you. (8) By this my Father is glorified, that you bear much fruit and so prove to be my disciples.**

We hear the "blank check" theology whereby we can ask anything from God and get it without any responsibility on our part. But what about the condition of abiding in the Son and having His Word abiding in us? One trait of the fruit of the disciple is that we bear much fruit for the glory of the Father. This fruit-bearing comes from the abiding process. The vine does not exist because of the branch. It is the branch that exists because of the vine. Our Lord Jesus Christ does not exist because of us. We exist because of our Lord Jesus Christ. Our life is found IN HIM!

> **John 15:1-2 ESV "I am the true vine, and my Father is the vinedresser. (2) Every branch in me that does not bear fruit he takes away, and every branch that does bear fruit he prunes, that it may bear more fruit.**

> **John 15:4-5 ESV Abide in me, and I in you. As the branch cannot bear fruit by itself, unless it abides in the vine, neither can you, unless you abide in me. (5) I am the vine; you are the branches. Whoever abides in me and I in him, he it is that bears much fruit, for apart from me you can do nothing.**

Taking the full context of these Scriptures should clear up the "blank check" mentality of many within the body. This "blank check" mentality seems driven by something other than a love for the Father and kingdom things.

A disciple is someone who continues in the Word of God and knows how to abide in His Word. The process of continuing in His Word will reveal truths that, in turn, will make us free. In fact, John chapter 8 is linked strongly to Romans chapter 6 (especially verses 6 and 16), and both chapters should be read to understand it completely. It would seem that some believers want the easy way and interpret something from a specific Scripture that the Scripture does not teach. This faulty interpretation causes the believer to run around claiming freedom only to find it did not work as advertised. So, the proper process of being free follows these steps: (1) Become a believer, (2) Be a person of the Word and learn to abide in it and let it abide in us, (3) Become a disciple, (4) Truths will be revealed that will make us free.

Being unteachable is one of the biggest obstacles to growing in maturity to discipleship. An old saying goes like this: "You can tell a Christian, but you can't tell him anything." This unteachable spirit shows itself when we are called to SUBMIT to the authority of God's Word and the spiritual leaders placed over us. One of the traits or fruits of "walking in the Spirit" from Ephesians 5:18 is submission to one another.

> **Ephesians 5:18-21 ESV And do not get drunk with wine, for that is debauchery, but be filled with the Spirit, (19) addressing one another in psalms and hymns and spiritual songs, singing and making melody to the Lord with your heart, (20) giving thanks always and for everything to God the Father in the name of our Lord Jesus Christ, (21) submitting to one another out of reverence for Christ.**

THE COST OF DISCIPLESHIP

Of course, rebellion, pride, and stubbornness are the opposite of submitting to one another. One statement I have heard repeated over and over for about thirty years concerning the obstinate attitude is, "many Christians are so full of pride they could strut sitting down." Being teachable is realizing we don't know it all and then choosing to walk with a spirit of brokenness and humility.

> *1 Peter 5:5-6 ESV Likewise, you who are younger, be subject to the elders. Clothe yourselves, all of you, with humility toward one another, for "God opposes the proud but gives grace to the humble." (6) Humble yourselves, therefore, under the mighty hand of God so that at the proper time he may exalt you,*
>
> *Hebrews 13:17 ESV Obey your leaders and submit to them, for they are keeping watch over your souls, as those who will have to give an account. Let them do this with joy and not with groaning, for that would be of no advantage to you.*
>
> *1 Thessalonians 5:12-13 ESV (12) We ask you, brothers, to respect those who labor among you and are over you in the Lord and admonish you, (13) and to esteem them very highly in love because of their work. Be at peace among yourselves.*
>
> *2 Thessalonians 3:14-15 ESV (14) If anyone does not obey what we say in this letter, take note of that person, and have nothing to do with him, that he may be ashamed. (15) Do not regard him as an enemy, but warn him as a brother.*

> *1 Peter 5:5-6 ESV Likewise, you who are younger, be subject to the elders. Clothe yourselves, all of you, with humility toward one another, for "God opposes the proud but gives grace to the humble." (6) Humble yourselves, therefore, under the mighty hand of God so that at the proper time he may exalt you,*

I had a sweet old Pastor years ago tell me that if someone taught or spoke something to you and you disagreed with 95% of it as being unscriptural, don't totally focus on the 95% of error but focus on the 5% of truth and allow God to teach you. I had some Pastors who disagreed with me concerning doctrinal differences years ago. I invited them to a round table discussion. I asked them to bring their Bibles because at least one of us or all of us may be wrong, and let's allow the iron to sharpen iron and learn from one another. We never reach a time in our ministry or our walk with the Lord that we know everything and should stop learning.

> *1 Corinthians 2:12-13 ESV (12) Now we have received not the spirit of the world, but the Spirit who is from God, that we might understand the things freely given us by God. (13) And we impart this in words not taught by human wisdom but taught by the Spirit, interpreting spiritual truths to those who are spiritual.*

> *Psalms 15:1-5 ESV A Psalm of David. O LORD, who shall sojourn in your tent? Who shall dwell on your holy hill? (2) He who walks blamelessly and does what is right and speaks truth in his heart; (3) who does not slander with his tongue*

> **and does no evil to his neighbor, nor takes up a reproach against his friend; (4) in whose eyes a vile person is despised, but who honors those who fear the LORD; who swears to his own hurt and does not change; (5) who does not put out his money at interest and does not take a bribe against the innocent. He who does these things shall never be moved.**

One of the simple truths that have been among the body of Christ for years and have been repeated many times goes like this, "we cannot take someone further spiritually than where we are." This statement is not a profound truth but let's look at the reality of our present day. We have more Churches and Pastors today than at any other time in history. We have more Christian TV stations, preaching, books, videos, and DVDs today than at any other time in history. We have more access to Christian teachings and ministries via the web or our phones than at any other time in history. Yet, with all of this mass media Christian influence worldwide, the cultures and societies are more corrupt, violent, and immoral than at any other time since the flood. What is going on? There is more mental head knowledge about God today than at any other time in history, but less teaching is taking place. WHY? To learn from someone teaching, we must have ears to hear what the Spirit and the Word are saying to us. To teach means that information is passed from one to another and received and applied. If a transfer of mental knowledge takes place without some change of life, it is hard to qualify that authentic teaching occurred. In our world, who is impacting who?

> *2 Timothy 2:1-2 ESV You then, my child, be strengthened by the grace that is in Christ Jesus, (2) and what you have heard from me in the presence of many witnesses entrust to faithful men who will be able to teach others also.*

Instead of teaching people the Word of God for life-changing results, we see a "people-pleasing message" released from the pulpits that tickle ears. A mother of one of the most well-known pastors in America was asked on a national TV program in 2011 why she thought her son was so famous worldwide. Without hesitation, she responded, "because he tells them what they want to hear." How sad is this? We need men of God like Paul, who spoke the hard truth to young Timothy and challenged him to faithfulness. We need to find believers who still have ears to hear the truth.

> *2 Timothy 1:13 ESV Follow the pattern of the sound words that you have heard from me, in the faith and love that are in Christ Jesus.*

> *2 Timothy 4:1-4 ESV I charge you in the presence of God and of Christ Jesus, who is to judge the living and the dead, and by his appearing and his kingdom: (2) preach the word; be ready in season and out of season; reprove, rebuke, and exhort, with complete patience and teaching. (3) For the time is coming when people will not endure sound teaching, but having itching ears they will accumulate for themselves teachers to suit their own passions, (4) and will turn away from listening to the truth and wander off into myths.*

THE COST OF DISCIPLESHIP

Acts 17:20-22 ESV For you bring some strange things to our ears. We wish to know therefore what these things mean." (21) Now all the Athenians and the foreigners who lived there would spend their time in nothing except telling or hearing something new. (22) So Paul, standing in the midst of the Areopagus, said: "Men of Athens, I perceive that in every way you are very religious.

Over the years of ministry, it has been observed that many Pastors, Bible teachers, and Christians will submit as long as the teaching agrees with their current mindset. In other words, many within the body of Christ already have their minds made up about what they believe and why they believe it. This attitude is good if the teaching is solidly grounded on the Word of God and nothing else. However, it may be doctrines that came from their past experiences, emotional ties, family members, denominational teachings, or mindsets developed by not rightly dividing the Word of God. If we are unwilling to pay the cost of being teachable by having ears to hear, how will we know if what we believe is solid Biblical doctrine?

Once a solid Biblical truth is taught that people disagree with, we see who really is teachable and wants to be a disciple versus those who just want their ears tickled. Unfortunately, we live in a "smorgasbord" and "buffet" mentality within Christianity, where believers feel they have the right to pick and choose what they want to believe and what they want to reject within the Scriptures.

I was reading an article from a well-known and respected Pastor who has been in the ministry for sixty years. He stated that he had been accused by those who deny the literal Word of God as being cultic and teaching heresy. His statement concerning the charges was basically what I have been saying. When people have their minds made up about what they believe and are unchangeable, they need to discredit those who challenged them with the Word. The easiest way to discredit someone when people don't want to learn from them is to accuse them of teaching heresy and call them cultic. Oh, how we need a teachable spirit within the body of Christ.

> ***Titus 2:1-5 ESV But as for you, teach what accords with sound doctrine. (2) Older men are to be sober-minded, dignified, self-controlled, sound in faith, in love, and in steadfastness. (3) Older women likewise are to be reverent in behavior, not slanderers or slaves to much wine. They are to teach what is good, (4) and so train the young women to love their husbands and children, (5) to be self-controlled, pure, working at home, kind, and submissive to their own husbands, that the word of God may not be reviled.***

Change only happens in our lives through the internalization of God's Word of Truth. But if we continue to believe what is comfortable and acceptable to us, we are guilty of doing what is right in our own eyes and will remain Christian babies. Our Lord Jesus Christ dealt with the religious leaders of His day in this area of religious dogma. We can all praise God for those Pastors who will not bow down under the pressure of the majority and will stand firm upon the Word of God no matter what cost is imposed upon them. We live in a day of tolerance and compromise, neither of which is pleasing to the Father. Sin is sin and will always be sin no matter what name we call it, and God will always hate it and judge it. The Word of God is faithful and will endure through the ages, no matter who believes it or denies it.

-10-
TO BE A DISCIPLE OF THE LORD JESUS CHRIST, THERE MUST BE A COMMITMENT TO TAKE ON THE YOKE OF OUR LORD JESUS CHRIST

Cost #1: Forsake Family Ties
Cost #2: Die To Self
Cost #3: Walk In Faithfulness
Cost #4: Love God And Others
Cost #5: A Spiritual Hunger And Thirst
Cost #6: Being Teachable
Cost #7: Take On The Yoke Of Christ

Matthew 11:28-30 ESV *Come to me, all who labor and are heavy laden, and I will give you rest. (29) Take my yoke upon you, and learn from me, for I am gentle and lowly in heart, and you will find rest for your souls. (30) For my yoke is easy, and my burden is light."*

In Matthew 11:29, "learn" comes from the Greek word used for a disciple. It could just as easily be translated as "Take my yoke upon you and become my disciple." Our Lord gave us two great natural symbols related to the attitude of commitment, and both were made of wood. The first was the *CROSS* which speaks to us as a symbol of submission. The second is the *YOKE* which speaks to us as a symbol of service. When we put the cross and yoke together, we get an accurate picture of

Biblical discipleship. A true disciple who has embraced the cross and the yoke will walk in submission and service.

By the way, it is important to remember that when an ox is fitted with a yoke to serve, his yoke does not work on another ox. The yoke wears a certain way across the shoulders of the ox and fits that ox something like one of our favorite shoes fit us. The way the yoke wears causes it not to fit on another ox whose size, shoulders, and muscles will differ. The same is true with the yoke the Lord has given us as disciples of service. We cannot place our yoke onto someone else, nor should we carry someone else's yoke.

As a Pastor, I could not count the number of times someone came up over the last forty-plus years and tried to fit me with their yoke. One man had tried to lay his conviction of an act of service on me, and I told him that it was his conviction, his yoke, and therefore he should do it. I actually had that man tell me that I was paid to do it. I informed him that I was a shepherd and not a hireling and that if he wanted to see that particular act of ministry and service done, he would be the one to do it. It never was accomplished. Why? He was a believer but not a disciple, and instead of becoming a disciple, he chose to place his yoke on someone else.

CLOSING REMARKS FROM THIS SECTION

The call of our Lord is a call to be a disciple. The cost is great, but the rewards are greater. GOD is more committed to us becoming a disciple than we are. However, the Father will stop the call when we no longer have ears to hear what the Spirit says.

Remember, to be a disciple of our Lord Jesus Christ; there must be a commitment…

- To forsake all family ties for Christ
- To dying to self
- To faithfulness
- To love the Lord Jesus Christ and the brothers
- To hunger and thirst for righteousness
- To being teachable
- To take on the yoke of Christ

-11-
THE COST OF DEVELOPING OTHERS INTO LEADERSHIP

We have looked at the cost of discipleship, but what about mentoring others? Many have asked me questions concerning the art of "MENTORING." The best thing to do is identify what mentoring is and who can do it. Mentorship is an art we all do from time to time, and we usually just call it "friendship." With a few "sometimes unknown" skills toned up, many of us would be great at mentoring. To begin, let's read some Scriptures on mentoring.

> *Proverbs 27:17 (ESV) Iron sharpens iron, and one man sharpens another.*
>
> *Isaiah 35:3-4 (ESV) Strengthen the weak hands, and make firm the feeble knees. 4 Say to those who have an anxious heart, "Be strong; fear not! Behold, your God will come with vengeance, with the recompense of God. He will come and save you."*
>
> *2 Timothy 2:3 (ESV) Share in suffering as a good soldier of Christ Jesus.*
> *Hebrews 10:24 (ESV)*
>
> *24 And let us consider how to stir up one another to love and good works,*

"MENTORING" typically is being…
1. A guide

2. A tutor
3. A coach
4. Or someone who influences another in life in both a profound and lasting way.

MENTORING is done through relationship, example, and service and involves giving resources such as time.

The basic practice of mentoring found in our society finds that the mentor and the protégé are within 5 or 6 years of being the same age. This closeness of age does not need to happen this way. However, people are greatly influenced by their friends, who also happen to be about their age. They are more than just friends, but "PEERS" who are mentoring one another. Early in our young relationships, we shared our dreams and hopes with friends. Then, as we shared, we found that some had similar goals and aspirations. With these, we learn to trust more and become more open about our deep desires. We found encouragement in this interaction and help in decision-making as we sought those dreams. As time passed, we became closer as we shared our heart's desires. The wisdom shared begins to sharpen each other through career changes, trials, and major life decisions.

What are the characteristics of a good or "ideal" mentor? What do I look for when I desire to be "raised" in maturity and wisdom to become a disciple of the Lord?

-12-
MARKS OF AN IDEAL MENTOR

What are we looking for when we desire to be a mentor or seek to find one? We certainly don't want to waste our time and find that the mentor we choose to follow is undisciplined or immature. What traits in word and deed can help us evaluate a proper mentor?

THE IDEAL MENTOR IS A PERSON WHO...

1. The ideal mentor is, first and foremost, a lover of God and His Word and bears his testimony of faith in word and deed.
2. The ideal mentor always seems to have what you need when you need it. The mentor has a prayer, a word, a hug, a rebuke, a suggestion, a shoulder, or a good listening ear.
3. The ideal mentor knows ways to cultivate relationships and draw people together.
4. The ideal mentor is willing to take a chance on you, and if you fail, he is ready to take another chance. They are eager to invest time, energy, talents, gifts, trust, and emotions in you and your well-being.
5. The ideal mentor is respected by other Christians and is someone you would not be bothered about walking a day in their shoes.
6. The ideal mentor may not have all the answers or resources but has a network whereby they can get the answer or help.
7. The ideal mentor is "sought out" by others for wisdom, information, or assistance.

8. The ideal mentor knows how to share their thoughts but also knows how to be a great listener.
9. The ideal mentor is consistent in their lifestyle. Before they "talk the talk," they "walk the walk."
10. The ideal mentor looks beyond the words you say and diagnoses your needs.
11. The ideal mentor is genuinely concerned with your interests and your maturity.

NOTE: The mentor is not necessarily a spiritual father or mother but can be. They are people who can meet our needs and sometimes are of the same age as we are. Due to the "experiences" and spiritual insight of some who are younger, we will find that they can bring a new level of wisdom, knowledge, and guidance to our lives. If the mentors are older spiritual fathers or mothers, we will tend to "give them the right" to speak into our lives more and for extended periods (some may do this for a lifetime).

-13-
HOW DO I FIND A MENTOR FOR ME

Finding a mentor will not be entirely left up to us. Why? We must desire to be mentored. There must be a willingness to come under a spiritual mom or dad to be discipled deeper than we are. We all have "blind" spots concerning our growth, maturity, and development. We may not see all the needs that we have.

Some disciples have developed a heart of compassion towards us that the Father prompted. They pray for us regularly in a particular way and desire to teach us and build a deeper relationship.

Realize that everyone in the faith can be of value in the mentoring process. Everyone has something to offer to us that will enrich of lives and cause us to change in wisdom, knowledge, and behavior.

The mentor protégé relationship should always be the same sex. This rule is not valid in the Pastoring relationship for the Pastor mentors through the preaching and teaching time to all people. But in a one-to-one relationship, we look for a mentor of our sex (males mentoring males and females mentoring females).

HOW LONG DO I NEED TO BE MENTORED

Mentoring is a "lifelong" process. We never get to the point where we can say that we cannot receive anything from anyone. The people who mentor us will change over the months or years, and the relationships established will remain deep and true. Never despise those who have labored among you the Word of truth.

1 Thessalonians 5:12-13 (ESV) We ask you, brothers, to respect those who labor among you and are over you in the Lord and admonish you, 13 and to esteem them very highly in love because of their work. Be at peace among yourselves.

We will change mentors according to the tasks at hand and the current needs of our lives. We all have a destiny to fulfill, and the Father will put those trained and mature in our lives for us to learn from. If not for mentoring, we all learn our way around by trial and error. We spend most of our lives trying something, and if it doesn't work, we try something else. In other words, we all keep reinventing the wheel. This process wastes time, energy, and resources and often results in a lifetime of pain and regret.

Example: We do not get a manual of operation when our children are born. The true principles of raising a child are within the Bible, but few know how to find and exercise those principles. In raising children, we only get a few chances to do it right with each child. If we fail, we stand the prospect of losing our children forever to the world and living in a broken relationship with them. So, instead of reinventing the wheel, would it be wise to look at parents who have been successful at child raising and ask them to mentor you in this area?

-14-
WHAT IS MY RESPONSIBILITY AS A TRAINEE OR "PROTÉGÉ"

Realize that the mentor to protégé relationship will not just happen. You must desire and seek it. You must be careful about your expectations. The mentor is not PERFECT, so give them room to fail and be human. Nor is the mentor GOD, so don't expect them to redeem you from a life mess instantly. There is also the chance of you expecting too little from the mentoring process. Expect a little bit, and you will get a little bit. The mentoring process takes time and effort. You and the mentor must be willing to invest in the process.
1. Set an agenda. Tell your mentor, "This is what I need assistance and growth in."
2. Test the advice/instruction given by the mentor with the Word of God and if proven true, then apply it.

NOTE: One of the most disheartening areas of a mentor is giving the same person the same instruction or advice over and over, realizing that they have no intention of applying it. It is a fact that some people want time from a person but not mentoring. Now, this is okay if that is established upfront. If someone just wants to "hang out" and chat, I can find time for that. But I would not give the time priority and effort as someone in a mentor protégé relationship. I am all about hanging out for coffee and fellowship, but it certainly will not carry the importance at the cost of discipling someone.

You and the mentor should have a JOINT agreement about the mentoring process. In that agreement, you give the mentor the right to speak into your life. When the time to change mentors comes, a JOINT agreement should be between you and your current mentor. You don't just drop the person and decide they are not suited for you anymore.

RESPONSIBILITIES OF THE MENTOR

After much prayer and leadership from the Lord, approach the person/persons you feel God has placed in your heart to mentor. DO NOT SAY, "God has told me to mentor you, so when do we meet?" Invite the person to your house and start the relationship-building process. Share that the Lord has placed them on your heart and that you have been praying for them. Ask if you can meet with them and pray and study together.

Remember that you are a man/woman of influence. As mentors, others will watch and hear what we do and say. Remember the things that we have to offer as mentors.

1. Experience: The skill of living.
2. Knowledge: Our area of expertise or books that we have read.
3. Access: To people, networks, and information.
4. Money: Luke 16:9 We are to use our money to advance the kingdom. This gift may mean everything in the life of our protégé.
5. Resources: Books, tools, furniture. We have acquired things that may meet a need in the life of the protégé.
6. Friendship: Offer companionship. The trip from boyhood to manhood is often lonely.
7. Time: The older we get, the busier we get, but the more control we have over our time. Make it a point to give some time to your protégé.

8. Ourself: There is nothing like giving of ourselves in a relationship. People want to know that we care enough to provide the best and genuinely love them.
9. God: The greatest resource we can give in a mentoring relationship is our faith in God. Sharing the characteristics of the Father's heart with a protégé will be the greatest asset we can leave someone with.

OTHERS MUST AUTHORIZE THE MINISTRY

A deep, personal relationship should be built between the mentor and the protégé. This relationship takes three key elements.
- TIME
- EFFORT
- THE RIGHT TO MINISTER

There are some points to remember when desiring to be mentored or desiring to mentor someone.

1. SELF-EXAMINATION: We must examine our lives to ensure that we are not doing or saying something that causes the protégé to say NO to us.
2. AUTHORITY: We must accept the fact that not everyone will authorize us to minister as their mentors. Do not take it personally, even if you believe you received a "Word" from the Lord about that person.
3. BOUNDARIES: Even those who allow us to mentor will often establish levels or boundaries of ministry. Be content to minister within those boundaries until deeper trust is established.
4. SETTING: Some will authorize us to mentor them ONLY in a group setting such as a pulpit, house church, or Bible study group.

5. OPENNESS: Some will allow you to minister and mentor one on one in a personal setting and allow you to minister to their soul and spirit.
6. CLOSURE: Those who allow us to minister or mentor them also have the right and authority to withdraw that right and authority.

It is always important that if someone withdraws from a ministry or mentoring relationship, you keep the lines of communication open and remain friends and continue to provoke a deeper relationship with the person.
- They may withdraw temporarily while they settle a personal issue.
- They may withdraw permanently.
- Remember that if someone withdraws from a ministry or mentoring relationship, it does not mean failure for either party.

-15-
DEALING WITH CONFLICT OR DISAGREEMENT IN THE MENTORING PROCESS

Some of the costs of discipleship is learning to face conflict and disagreement between you, the leader, and the protégé. I wish I could tell you it won't happen to you, but I can't. The closest of friends in the mentor relationship could split over issues that may never be defined. The protégé might come under a spiritual attack where his mind is filled with lies and accusations against the mentor. One day unexpectedly, it all comes out and blindsides the mentor. The forces behind the mentor protégé discipling process are great. All involved must be keenly aware that praying together in a warfare position is necessary for the discipling team.

Not all conflict is necessarily bad. The conflict may shed new light on the heart of both the mentor and the protégé. However, the dispute must remain focused. Remember that we are Christian brothers and sisters and are to love one another and hate sin.

DEALING WITH CONFLICT

1. Anticipate that there are going to be controversial topics that will arise in the mentoring process.
2. Ensure that the mentor and protégé relationship has grown so that it can handle controversial issues before you attempt to deal with them.
3. Don't avoid dealing with controversial topics if you know the relationship can withstand them.

4. Be sure that you have facts related to the topic from the Word of God.
5. Be able to recognize and discern conflict as it is starting.
6. Conflict almost always starts as a result of the feeling of confusion or the feeling of rejection.
7. Conflict usually starts in the relationship when one or both in the mentoring process feel attacked in their thoughts or emotions.
8. Keep the topic clear in the mentor/protégé relationship, and be careful of chasing rabbits or adding other issues to the fire.
9. Clarify obscure Scriptures on the topic if possible.
10. Clarify obscure statements from one another.
11. You might ask this question to ensure that what you heard is what the other person said, "Is this what you are trying to express?" Or you could try this method, "Let me see if I get what you mean."
12. Acquire sensitivity to the mood and temper of the other person/persons within the mentoring/protégé process. Be compassionate.
13. Listen for the "EMOTIONALLY charged" phases.
14. Add positive behavior within the relationship to disarm the conflict.
15. Keep the attitude of humility and that we, as dead people, don't have the right to be right.
16. Focus on the areas of conflict where both parties agree.
17. Use humor, if possible, to discharge emotional tension.
18. STOP EVERYTHING AND PRAY TOGETHER.

-16-
HOW TO MAKE THE TIME YOU NEED

Yes, that's right, we can make the time to do what we need to do. We don't wait until we HAVE the time to disciple people. We choose to MAKE the time to disciple.

Not having time to do the ETERNAL things is not an excuse we can use with the Father. He has given us all the time we need to accomplish what He has placed in our hands. We may not have the time to do our thing, so we must choose what we will do with our time and which KINGDOM we will invest in.

As we get older, we realize the greatest commodity we possess is our time. Since it is our most precious possession, we must be faithful with our time by using it wisely. What better way to use our time than to pour our lives into others? We must seek to leave the next generation better by sowing into it. We must be diligent in sowing God's Word into the spiritual children the Father has given us to mentor.

> **Psalms 78:2-4 (ESV) I will open my mouth in a parable; I will utter dark sayings from of old, 3 things that we have heard and known, that our fathers have told us. 4 We will not hide them from their children, but tell to the coming generation the glorious deeds of the LORD, and his might, and the wonders that he has done.**

The next generation needs to know the mighty works of our Lord. As the days become more wicked and lawless, there is hope that we can pass on to the hopeless.

> **Psalms 78:6-7 (ESV) that the next generation might know them, the children yet unborn, and arise and tell them to their children, 7 so that they should set their hope in God and not forget the works of God, but keep his commandments;**

The cost of discipleship is great. However, the cost of not discipling young believers carries a higher price. We didn't wake up one day, and our nation turned rebellious and lawless. This lawlessness happened one failed or improper mentorship at a time. If we do not give the next generation Jesus Christ and Him crucified, the wicked are ready to mentor the next generation into even more wickedness.

> **Psalms 78:8 (ESV) and that they should not be like their fathers, a stubborn and rebellious generation, a generation whose heart was not steadfast, whose spirit was not faithful to God.**

FACTS ABOUT TIME:

Here are some facts about time as we invest our lives into others. We must be time-savers if we are going to mentor people.
- Time is a neutral commodity
- Time does not have a soul. Time does not have a personality. Time cannot think or feel. Therefore, time cannot choose. We make a choice.

- The value of time varies according to SUPPLY and DEMAND. If I spend all my time on the world's demands, I have devalued time to WORTHLESSNESS. If I use my time to advance the kingdom and on eternal things, then my time is PRICELESS.
- I control my time, outside forces control my time, or my time controls me.
- Time can be wasted or lost. It is wasted or lost by getting a late start on something. Some are always late because they waste or lose time.
- Personal habits can become rituals. Just because we have "always" been a certain way does not mean that it is RIGHT and that we always must be that way! We can develop bad habits that are time robbers and find ourselves a slave to our rituals.
- If we can develop bad habits of wasting time, we can also develop good habits of saving time.
- Many waste time by quitting too early at the end of the day. Our early forefathers worked 12 to 14 hours daily from sun-up to sundown. Many of us today have been spoiled and feel like we have put in a day's work if we work 6 hours.
- Procrastination. Don't do today what we can put off until tomorrow. Procrastination can rob us of valuable time and energy. Putting things off until later or procrastination causes a pile-up of small jobs until it takes more time to organize the mess we have created than it would have been just to do the small jobs as they arise.
- Lack of planning. There is a motto that has been a part of the military for as long as I can remember. It says, "Work smarter and not harder." It is not advocating that we don't work hard, but that we plan our work to get it done in the best time and energy-saving method.

- Failure to concentrate. One of Debby's favorite messages to me when I get too busy is, "be present where you are." If I am driving and don't concentrate, it never fails that I miss my turn and have to find a place to turn around. This detour, of course, results in a loss of time and gas. Think about what you are doing or going to do.

THE BEST WAYS TO MANAGE YOUR TIME.

1. We must recognize priorities.

Remember this statement: "I will do everything I deem important today." I may not do everything that I need to do, but those things that I prioritize are the things that I will do.

If I did not pray, read my Bible, mentor someone, or have fellowship with Christian brothers and sisters, it was because I did not deem them as priorities for my day. Don't say, "Well, I wanted to." Life is filled with good intentions yet bad planning.

Suppose I did nothing today. It is because I did what I thought was important today, which is NOTHING. So, it is wise to list those things we need to do the night before or early in the morning so that I can prioritize them. Priority #1 is things that I must get done that day. Priority #2 is things that I strongly want to do that day. Priority #3 is things that, if I get to today, that will be great, but it is something that can wait.

2. We must plan the Day's work agenda.

If you are traveling, try making all the trips together to save time and gas. Set up your meetings with your protégés so you have time between them to accomplish a task. Determine how long the tasks that need to be completed today will take and plan accordingly.

As an author, I must decide how many pages I want to type each day to complete a book at the time I set for completion. If I want to write a 100-page book and have it completed in one month, I must type at least three pages daily. I also must determine the best time to type with the least number of disturbances. Since I receive many phone calls and messages during the day, I know that my best time to write is before 8 am. Therefore, I get up between 4-5 each morning to type. I also need to plan the rest of my day accordingly to keep my time from being hacked by unnecessary distractions. I should not have to have my day thrown in chaos trying to do what I had planned just because others don't know how to plan and use their time wisely.

3. We need to delegate to others all matters possible.

Delegating is for at least two key reasons.
- We cannot do everything. Therefore, the more projects we try to do in a single day, the more we lose quality. We find ourselves gaining acceptance of how many things we control.
- We rob others of growing emotionally, intellectually, and spiritually if we do all the work. We deprive others of exercising their gifts and talents and cause everyone to depend on us.

4. We need to start to work early.

When I can get started typing and studying early, I am always amazed at how much I complete in those first couple hours. Then as the day goes on, my tasks compete with visits, phone calls, and of course, "honey-dos." ("Honey-dos" are those things that our spouse desires us to do. Honey, do this, and honey, do that).

5. We need to solve one problem at a time.

It is emotionally and intellectually draining to try to work on a multitude of issues at the same time. Put a priority on them and solve them one at a time.

6. We must concentrate on the task at hand.

Don't lose time thinking about your next job while in the middle of this one. It will cause a loss in a step or miscommunication and result in doing work over again.

7. We should plan relaxation periods.

The more meticulous the task, the more we require taking a break and walk away from it for a few minutes. Take a walk outside and breath some fresh air.

8. We need to be "time conscious."

Don't start a task you know you cannot complete and will have to start from the beginning of the next day. If you are on the phone, be aware that the phone eats hours each day from people in needless conversation. Set a time limit for your phone calls. Be time conscious on breaks, etc.

Pray that God will use you to redeem the time for the days are evil. Pray that the Father will give you the wisdom to use time wisely and for His glory.

THE COST OF DISCIPLESHIP

The cost of discipleship. We can put it all into one statement. It will cost you your life. Is it worth it? Our Lord Jesus thought so as He poured His life into the twelve, even knowing that one would betray Him. The Apostle Paul thought the mentoring process was worth it as He mentored many, including young Timothy.

> **2 Timothy 2:2 (ESV) and what you have heard from me in the presence of many witnesses entrust to faithful men, who will be able to teach others also.**

> **1 Timothy 4:6 (ESV) If you put these things before the brothers, you will be a good servant of Christ Jesus, being trained in the words of the faith and of the good doctrine that you have followed.**

Find your one; hopefully, you will catch the compassion and calling to find your twelve. Reproduce yourself in someone. Leave your mark so that long after you leave this mortal world, your words will echo in the hearts of those you touched. Discipleship. Is it worth it? You can bet on it.

MORE BOOKS BY CHARLES MORRIS

Look for eBooks (EB), paperbacks (PB), & hardcovers (HC)

1. **THE FOUR POSITIONS OF THE HOLY SPIRIT**: Beside Us, Within Us, Upon Us, and Filling Us (EB, PB, HC) (2014 02 17; 2021 10 02, 1st, 2nd, & 3rd Editions).
2. **BORN AGAIN:** Having a Personal Relationship with God (EB, PB, HC) (2021 07 09, 1st & 2nd Editions).
3. **THE 10 CHARACTERISTICS OF A SPIRIT-FILLED CHURCH:** The Spirit-Filled Life Bible Study (EB, PB, 1st Edition).
4. **THE COVENANT OF SALT:** Everyone Will be Salted with Fire (EB, PB, HC) (2021 10 03, 1st Edition).
5. **THE PARABLE OF THE FOUR SOILS:** The Key to the Mystery of the Kingdom of God. (EB, PB, HC) (2021 06 23, 1st Edition).
6. **THE FIVE EVIDENCES OF SALVATION:** How Do I Know That I'm Saved. (EB, PB, HC) (2021 09 10, 1st & 2nd Editions).
7. **FAITHFUL:** How Can I Be Faithful to God? (EB, PB, HC) (2021 06 20, 1st & 2nd Editions).
8. **HOSEA:** What Does the Book of Hosea Teach Us? (EB, PB, HC) (2021 05 28, 1st Edition).
9. **PREPARING OURSELVES TO HEAR THE VOICE OF GOD:** Do You Want to Hear the Voice of God? Book 1 (EB, PB, HC) (2021 06 09, 1st & 2nd Editions).
10. **FIFTEEN WAYS TO HEAR THE VOICE OF GOD:** Do You Want to Hear the Voice of God? Book 2. (EB, PB, HC) (2021 06 11, 1st & 2nd Editions).
11. **THE 24 QUALIFICATIONS OF AN ELDER:** What Are the Biblical Requirements to Be an Elder? (EB,

PB, HC) (2021 07 03, 1st Edition).
12. **THE BIBLE PROVES ITSELF TRUE** (EB, PB, HC) (2021 09 03, 1st Edition).
13. **EXPERIENCING THE BEAUTY OF BROKENNESS:** You Shall Be a Crown of Beauty in the Hand of the Lord, and a Royal Diadem in the Hand of Your God (EB, PB, 1st Edition).
14. **PLACES WHERE GOD AND MAN MEET:** A Guide to Worshipping in Spirit & Truth (EB, PB, HC) (2021 09 25, 1st Edition).
15. **YOUR DASH:** Writing Your Life Journal (PB, 1st & 2nd Edition).
16. **CHART YOUR PATH**: Bible Study Journal (PB, 1st & 2nd Editions).
17. **THE FIVE WITNESSES OF SALVATION:** You Shall Know The By Their Fruit. (EB, PB, HC, 1st Edition).
18. **HOW DO I WRITE A BOOK?** From Passion to Paper to Print (EB, PB, 1st Edition).
19. **HOSEA INTRODUCTION:** Can You Still Hear the Call? (EB, 1st Edition).
20. **HOSEA 1:1-3:** The Divine Command to Marry Gomer. (EB, 1st Edition).
21. **HOSEA 1:4-5:** A Marriage, A Son, and the Promise of Judgment. (EB, 1st Edition).
22. **HOSEA 1:6-7:** A Daughter, an Unfaithful Wife, Heartbreak, and No Mercy (EB, 1st Edition).
23. **HOSEA 1:8-9:** A Son, You Are Not My People, I Am Not Your God. (EB, 1st Edition).
24. **HOSEA 1:10-11:** The Ultimate Promise: Divine Intervention And Restoration. (EB, 1st Edition).
25. **A WILLINGNESS TO BE TAUGHT:** Overcoming The Dull Of Hearing Syndrome. (EB, PB, HC) (2021 12 03, 1st Edition).
26. **LUKE 15:** The Sheep, A Wandering Heart; The Coin, A Careless Heart; The Son, A Rebellious Heart. (EB, PB, 1st Edition).

27. ***THE MYSTERY OF LAWLESSNESS UNLEASED.*** (EB, PB, HC, 1st Edition).
28. ***THE CHRONOLOGICAL BOOK OF END TIMES:*** 11 Undeniable Prophecies Of The End Times. (EB, PB, HC) (2022 03 16, 1st Edition).
29. ***IS ATHEISM DEAD?***: The Unbelieving Unbelievers Epidemic. Book 1 of the "They Walk Among Us" series. (EB, PB, HC) (2022 03 01, 1st Edition).
30. ***WHEREVER YOU GO TRAVEL JOURNAL:*** The Ultimate Guide To All 50 States. (PB, 1st Edition).
31. ***WHEREVER YOU GO TRAVEL JOURNAL (FOR TEENS):*** The Ultimate Guide To All 50 States. (PB, 1st Edition).
32. ***THE TOPICAL JOURNAL:*** Journal Like A Veteran (PB 1st Edition).
33. ***THE TOPICAL JOURNAL:*** Don't Just Sit There, JOURNAL. For women. (PB, 1st Edition).
34. ***THE TOPICAL JOURNAL:*** Journaling That Impacts Your Life. (PB, 1st Edition). PB 1st Edition.
35. ***WHEREVER YOU GO TRAVEL JOURNAL (FOR THE GUYS):*** The Ultimate Guide to All 50 States. (PB, 1st Edition).
36. ***THE TOPICAL JOURNAL:*** Don't Just Sit There, Journal. For Men. (PB, 1st Edition).
37. ***IS RELIGION DEAD?:*** The Believing Unbelievers Epidemic. Book 2 of the "They Walk Among Us" series. (EB, PB, HC) (2022 06 18, 1st Edition).
38. ***UNLEASHED: Understanding The Mystery Of Lawlessness.*** (EB, PB, HC) (2022 06 26, 1st Edition).
39. ***I FEEL LIKE I'M LOSING MY FAITH:*** How Do I Fix My Faulty Faith? (EB, PB, 1st Edition).
40. ***WE NEED FAITH:*** Faith After Doubt. (EB, PB, HC) (2022 07 25, 1st Edition).
41. ***THE HOLY BIBLE THE KING JAMES VERSION OF THE OLD AND NEW TESTAMENTS -ANNOTATED-:*** (EB 2022 08 06)

42. IS CHRISTIAN IMMATURITY DEAD?: The Unbelieving Believers Epidemic. Book 3 of the "They Walk Among Us" series. (EB, PB, HC) (2022 09 02, 1st Edition).

43. THE PARABLE OF THE WHEAT AND TARES: A Guide To Understanding The Kingdom Of God (EB, PB, HC) (2022 10 08, 1st Edition)

44. GO TELL IT ON THE MOUNTAIN: The Great Commission, God's Plan To Reach The World. (EB, PB, HC) (2022 11 17, 1st Edition)

Charles W Morris

ABOUT THE AUTHOR

Over the last 45 years, CHARLES MORRIS has served God and the body of Christ as a pastor, church planter, evangelist, house church ministry coordinator, and author of over 40 books. He is also the founder and CEO of RSIM (Raising the Standard International Ministry), RSIP (Raising the Standard International Publishing LLC), and RSISoM (Raising the Standard International School of Ministry).

Pastor Charles has devoted his life, talents, gifts, and resources to call the church back to the place of walking in God's holiness in the power and Person of the Holy Spirit. He calls on the church, the living body of Christ on the earth, to live daily by God's standards of being Christ-like in word, deed, and thought.

Pastor Charles believes the Bible teaches that it is paramount that all who confess to knowing Christ have full assurance that they are genuinely saved by examining their lives according to the standards set within the Word of God. After proof of salvation, he also believes all Christians should seek baptism with the Holy Spirit to be a bold witness for our Lord Jesus Christ across the street and to the ends of the earth. Charles currently lives with his wife, Debra, in Navarre, Florida.

www.ingramcontent.com/pod-product-compliance
Lightning Source LLC
Chambersburg PA
CBHW071729160125
20485CB00030B/530